HAVE YOU COME FAR?

HAVE YOU COME FAR?

A LIFE IN INTERVIEWS

VAUGHAN GRYLLS

WILMINGTON SQUARE BOOKS
an imprint of Bitter Lemon Press

WILMINGTON SQUARE BOOKS
An imprint of Bitter Lemon Press

First published in 2018 by
Wilmington Square Books
47 Wilmington Square
London WC1X 0ET

www.bitterlemonpress.com

A CIP record for this book is available from the British Library

ISBN 978-1-9122421-4-6

2 4 6 8 9 7 5 3 1

Designed and typeset by Jane Havell Associates
Printed by TJ International, Padstow

THOSE INTERVIEWS

INTRODUCTION

I'm a 74-year-old artist and photographer but before that I taught in art colleges and universities for years and years, ending up actually running one.

The thing is I've had more interviews – and of every type going – than most. Here you will find snooty interviews, crude interviews, rude interviews, interviews for the sack and even an interview that never took place. So I thought, seeing as nearly everyone will at some time in their lives have an interview, it would be fun to share some of mine with you. At least, you could then know what not to do.

It is often said that a good interview is a two-way affair where interviewers and interviewee find out about one another. Well, maybe, but really any interview is a pretty hit-and-miss affair with a huge amount of luck involved. As for the interviewer, they will never know whether they have made the right choice until the chosen one turns up and does or doesn't do the job they wanted done.

I would like to thank my brother, David Grylls, for reading my draft and suggesting its title, Peter Kemp for some valuable suggestions and Ferdy Carabott for getting my prose in order. I would also like to thank my publisher, John Nicoll, for his sterling support.

In the interests of avoiding legal action arising from my descriptions of some of the interviews suffered, I have sometimes invented the names of the interviewers and the titles of the organisations they represented. Other than that, all you read here is true.

I do hope you find this lifetime's experience of being grilled entertaining and even of some use, whether you are an interviewee, an interviewer or both.

VAUGHAN GRYLLS
Uphousden, Kent 2018

ST PAUL'S CATHEDRAL CHOIR SCHOOL, 1951

My first interview took place when I was just seven. My mother had found out from the organist of her local church that if a boy could sing and he got into a cathedral choir school, when his voice broke he could be transferred to a public school with the fees waived. The recommended example was St Paul's Cathedral Choir School with onward progression supplied by St Paul's School or Dulwich College. I've no idea if this was true, but what I do know is that one day an ancient piano arrived at our house, not for me to learn to play but for me to learn to sing at, under the instruction of the organist who had first advised her . . .

Knock.

"Come in! It's open!"

Push at a very big door. Now in a very big room and I'm shaking . . . Close door behind you . . . Don't drop that sheet music tucked under your arm.

"That's it. Don't be afraid!"

Two men behind a big desk. The one who I think told me to come in leans forward. The other doesn't move. He is leaning back with his hands clasped behind his head. Obviously he doesn't care whether I get in or not.

"Hello! Grylls isn't it? Vaughan Grylls?" says the leaning forward one.

"Yes. That is my name."

"Splendid. Thank you for coming. How old are you, Grylls?"

"Seven. But I'm eight at Christmas. December the tenth actually."

"Splendid. Well, I'm the Headmaster of the Choir School. And this is our Choirmaster. The exam wasn't too bad, was it?"

"Er, no sir."

"Splendid. Well, the Choirmaster will play each piece of music you have chosen through once and then you can let us hear you sing along to each piece as he accompanies you. Does that sound pretty reasonable?"

"Yes sir."

"Splendid. Those must be your music scores?"

"Yes sir."

"Well, hand them over then! Let us take a peek."

Walk up to the desk and do as you are told. And try and stop shaking.

"Now, before we do any singing, it would be a good idea if we had a little chat, don't you think? So do sit down."

There is only one place to sit – a solitary chair right in front of the desk. I scramble up.

"Good. Well now. Have you come far?"

The Headmaster glances down at a paper on his desk. Before I have time to reply he looks up.

"I see you've come quite a long way, Grylls. Newark on Trent?"

"Yes sir."

"Splendid. Good journey. To King's Cross?"

"No. To London."

"King's Cross. It's a railway station in London. Trains go through Newark to King's Cross. From places like Edinburgh. So . . . we have to assume you didn't walk all the way . . . like Dick Whittington and his cat?"

He chuckles. I look down, shake my head and smile to myself in embarrassment.

"Now. That's more like it. We are not going to eat you, you know. So how did you get here?"

"I came by car, with my mother and father."

"Splendid. Down the Great North Road no less. Tell us something about your journey."

"Er, well it took all day. It is an old car you see and, well, we had to keep stopping to let the engine cool down. But it got to London in the end."

The old car. This is a bit embarrassing. Why did I say that?

"Well, you, mum and dad and the old car all arrived! That is the main thing, what? So. Tell us a little about where you stopped and what you saw?"

"We stopped at a pub . . . where a highwayman once slept."

"Ah, Dick Turpin, I would bet? But you couldn't go into the pub at your age, could you?"

"No, of course not."

What a silly thing to ask. Surely he knows that.

"So what did you do?"

"I sat in the car with a packet of crisps while it cooled down and . . ."

"And Mummy and Daddy were inside the pub cooling down themselves, what?"

The Headmaster turns to the Choirmaster. They grin at one other. Why is this so funny?

"And then?"

"After that we stopped at the side of the road – actually in a track where a tractor goes into a field and we had our sandwiches and I ran round the field a bit. Father said we had just driven across the smallest county in the country. It is called Rutland, he said."

"Good memory. Well done. And then what?"

"A petrol station. We stopped there. The other cars were a Jaguar and an Armstrong Siddeley. Our car is about the oldest and slowest on the road. Everybody overtook us apart from some lorries. It is an Austin 10. It was made in 1936."

"Well, when you grow up, you will just have to own a big, fast car yourself, won't you? What do you fancy?"

"Er, maybe a Bristol."

"Hmm. Very stylish. They are actually built in Bristol, you know. Now, what else did you see. On your journey?"

"We drove to look around a model village. It was in Letchworth. It was very interesting. The tops of the houses were a bit lower than me. It was like, being in [oh dear, have they heard of this?] . . . *Gulliver's Travels.*"

"Splendid. And apt. Did you know Gulliver was a native of Newark?"

"No. I thought the book was made up."

"Of course it was made up. But Dean Swift, its author, decided his hero should be a native of Newark."

"Oh. I didn't read that bit."

"Don't worry. You probably read a children's version."

Now I do worry. A children's version? They must think I am babyish. I shall try and change the subject.

"We eventually got to London. We drove down Highgate Hill and Father pointed out the dome of St Paul's. You could see it in the distance."

"Splendid. We do stand out rather."

Both men are now leaning forward.

What else can I say? I've got to remember the other things . . .

"It is the tallest building in London. 365 feet. One foot for every day of the year. It was designed by Sir Christopher Wren."

"Indeed. Well remembered, Grylls. But sadly it doesn't get a foot taller every fourth year."

Fourth year? Taller? What is he talking about?

"You look puzzled. A leap year, Grylls!"

Oh, I get it. He is making a joke like something out of *Alice*. All right. Here goes.

"It could get a foot taller if it was in *Alice In Wonderland*. I liked that book."

"Yes. So do we all. Now. What do you think of our school? You've been up to our rooftop playground, haven't you? After your exam."

"Yes. I've never been to one on a roof before. It was fun looking down on all the buildings. Especially St Paul's nearby . . . which was taller of course."

Thought I'd better add that in.

"Yes, at least 300 feet taller . . . What else did you see?"

"Well, a lot of broken buildings."

"Bombed buildings?"

"Yes. But they are building new ones with cranes and things . . . it will look better soon."

I'm trying to make them like me.

"Let us hope so, Grylls. The Cathedral was bombed you know. But not badly, thank the Lord. Have you been inside with Mummy and Daddy?"

They are never called Mummy and Daddy. It is Mother and Father.

"I have been inside with my mother and my father. Yesterday afternoon."

"Splendid."

"It's the biggest place I've ever been in. I would have liked to . . ."

"Sing in it! Of course. Let us hope you will be able to."

"Well, actually, I meant to have built it. From a drawing I would have made."

Now the Choirmaster and Headmaster turn to look at one another. Then back to me.

"Ha ha ha! Well, before you start designing us a new St Paul's, Grylls, why don't we hear you sing. Geoffrey, are you all right with those scores?"

"Yes Headmaster. Quite all right."

The Choirmaster rises and waves his hand towards a grand piano in the corner.

"Come along Grylls. Lets have a crack at these, shall we?"

Clamber out of my seat and traipse behind the choirmaster across the vast room. The headmaster stays put, pushes his chair back, moves his glasses to his forehead and lights a cigarette. This is going to be the most terrifying bit.

"Let's start with your little Schubert shall we? *Heidenroslein.*"

"Er, which?"

"*Rose among the Heather.* Come and stand by the piano next to me and face the Headmaster. I"ll play it through first.

"Right. There it is. A pretty piece. Are you singing it in the original?

"Original."

"German. Did you know that?"

"No sir."

"Fine. So sing it in English. Hear we go."

> *A boy saw a rose,*
> *A rose on the heather,*
> *It was young and beautiful as the morning,*
> *He ran to get a better look*
> *And viewed it with joy.*
> *Rose, rose, red rose,*

Rose on the heather.
The boy said, "I'm going to pick you,
Rose on the heather."
The rose said, "I"ll prick you,
So that you'll always remember me,
And I will not let you."
Rose, rose, red rose . . . Rose on the heather.
And the wild boy picked
The rose on the heather;
The rose fought back and pricked him,
But the pain did no good, and oh,
Such suffering must happen.
Rose, rose, red rose.
Rose on the heather.

Slow, loud clapping from behind a cloud of cigarette smoke. The Choirmaster switches the music sheets.

"Now, Grylls. Your second piece. Franz Lehar no less. I'm sure you will produce a wonderful Richard Tauber impression for us – treble version of course!"

What is he talking about?

"Don't look puzzled. I"ll play it through once and then you can go straight in. This should be fun. So off I go . . ."

I don't care what is fun and what isn't. All I can do is sing as loudly and as best I can . . .

Girls were made to love and kiss
And who am I to interfere with this?
Is it well? Who can tell?
But I know the good Lord made it so
Am I ashamed to follow nature's way?
Shall I be blamed if God has made me gay?
Does it pay? Who can say?
I'm a man and kiss her when I can
Yet I have suffered in love's great deeps
I know the passion that never sleeps

I know the longing and wronging of hearts
The hope that flatters and shatters and smarts
I suffer still but I sleep at nights
Man cannot always be on the heights
And when our aching and breaking is done
Flirting is jolly, it's folly, but fun
Girls were made to love and kiss
And who am I to interfere with this?
Does it pay? Who can say?
I'm a man and kiss her when I can.

More slow, loud clapping from the Headmaster but this time the Choirmaster joins in.

"A little bow perhaps – towards the audience – me!" says the Headmaster.

I oblige. More clapping.

"Geoffrey. I think the Dean would absolutely love this. Could you just pop out and see if he is still in his study?"

The Choirmaster jumps up from the piano stool and heads for the door.

"I"ll be as quick as I can, Headmaster."

"Thank you Geoffrey. So tell me. Your uniform."

He glances down again at the paper on his desk.

"Newark Preparatory School. Be Prepared."

"Prepared?"

"It is written on your pocket badge, Grylls. Where are you staying in London? Friends, relatives?"

"No. We don't have any. We are staying at a hotel."

"Do you know where?"

"Russell, Russell . . ."

"The Russell Hotel. Oh very big and smart."

"No, it is not big. It is near there, I think, because Father said he will remember it is near there the next time."

"The next time?"

"Well, you see, yesterday, Father had to leave us at the hotel while he went to park the car a long way away and he was gone a long time and so

Mother started getting worried and when he came back he looked very worried and red in the face as he couldn't find his way back to the hotel as he had forgotten what it was called. Mother seemed to have gone white in the face when he was away so long."

"Red and white. Oh dear. Poor chap. And your worried mother."

Why have I told him about this and the old car and . . .

The door swings open. A man with white hair wearing a black suit and a clergyman's collar followed by the Choirmaster. The Headmaster jumps up from his desk.

"May I introduce you to the Very Reverend Matthews who is in charge of the Cathedral? This is Master Vaughan Grylls, Mr Dean."

The Dean smiles and moves over to shake my hand.

"I hear you are going to sing something for me. *Girls were made to love and kiss,* no less."

I didn't know I was going to sing but the Choirmaster has already moved back to the piano stool and he has now started playing. Oh no. And the Headmaster is back behind his desk lighting another cigarette. As for the Dean, he is now standing in the middle of the room with his arms folded.

> *Girls were made to love and kiss*
> *And who am I to interfere with this?*
> *Is it well? Who can tell?*
> *But I know the good Lord made it so*

I was offered a place but they didn't put up with me for long, as I started wetting the bed. So I was transferred to my local cathedral choir school at Southwell Minster, Nottinghamshire, where I stayed until I failed the eleven plus for the Southwell Minster Grammar School.

SKEGNESS SECONDARY MODERN SCHOOL, 1955

After I failed the eleven plus, my parents did not know what to do with me. Even if they had the money, which they didn't, they could not send me to a private boarding school as I still wet the bed and, in any case, there were none within daily travelling distance. One day my father said he had found that it was easier to get a transfer to a grammar school in Lincolnshire than to one in Nottinghamshire, where we lived. So they looked at a secondary modern at North Hykeham, just outside Lincoln. It was only fifteen miles away from Newark so I could travel by bus daily. But Lincolnshire Education Authority said no. If you wished to attend a state school in Lincolnshire, you had to live in the county. So my mother had a brainwave. I could go and live where we spent our summer holidays – Auntie Irene's house, near Skegness.

My mother turns and shouts, "I think you'll like it here, Vaughan. It looks very nice." And then back to her sister, "Don't you think so, Rene?"

My mother, Auntie Irene and I are traipsing across a windswept playground towards the centre of a red-brick single-storey building. At its far end is a flagpole. I bet they fly the Union Jack from that on Empire Day, just like they did at Southwell Minster. The only thing that's the same.

"Come on, Vaughan."

"I'm coming. My shoelace has come undone."

"Well, do it up then. Hurry up. They said twelve o clock."

I attend to the laces, hands trembling. We have come from Chapel St Leonards about eight miles away where Auntie Irene lives, and we have just got off a Lincolnshire Road Car Company double-decker bus. I can't believe I have come to this.

"Come on, Vaughan. Make out as though you're interested. They may be looking at us."

I look up and then make an effort at running. There are no children about. They are in the classrooms which surround the playground on three sides. I can see them through the windows.

"Well, Mr Bannister. Vaughan would love to join your school. Wouldn't you, Vaughan?"

The Headmaster looks me up and down.

"I'm sure he would. Why would you like to come here?"

"Er, well . . ."

"He wants to live at Chapel St Leonards. Fresh air. We come on holiday here every year."

"No, please let your son answer himself, Mrs Grylls."

"Er, it is true. I'll like it."

"And you, Mrs Wall. I asked you to come along to vouch for the fact that your nephew will be living with you. Not being from Lincolnshire we have to establish his new domicile."

"Yes. No, Vaughan will love it with me. Won't you, Vaughan?"

I nod at Auntie Irene and look back at my shoes. Now the other lace has come undone.

"Well, Mrs Grylls. I think that is all. I will show you the class your son will be joining and he can then stay here for the rest of this afternoon. Can you collect him at a quarter to four?"

My mother glances across at Auntie Irene.

"We'll go to The Sun Castle, Rene. And then decide what to do."

Auntie Irene nods. She always agrees with everything my mother says. Actually, everybody does.

"Good." Mr Bannister leans back, closes his eyes and puts his hands together like a church steeple.

"Is there anything else you would like to ask or let me know about, Mrs Grylls?"

"Is there a uniform, Mr Bannister?"

"No. I'm afraid not."

"So would it be all right for Vaughan to wear these clothes? I'll take the badge off, of course."

The Head opens his eyes.

"The badge?"

"Yes, it's his Southwell Minster uniform. It'll be the same but with the badge on the pocket taken off."

"Ah yes. A bishop's mitre. Nice badge. You were at Southwell Minster, weren't you? But you didn't pass your eleven plus."

I nod and look down at my shoes again. Shall I tie that lace? Everything falling apart. I must not cry.

"Vaughan is a cathedral chorister, Mr Bannister. Got into St Paul's in London. And then Southwell Minster. Could he sing here properly?"

"I'm sure he could, Mrs Grylls. If it happens that our music mistress arranges a choir."

"And that is all?"

"I'm afraid so, Mrs Grylls. I doubt the Church of England will be building a cathedral in Skegness in the near future, if at all. If they did, I'm sure your son's voice would have broken by the time it was completed."

Mr Bannister smiles bleakly. He places his hands together again, emphasising the mockery.

Lincolnshire Road Car Co. Ltd.

"Did you think some of those children were a bit common, Rene?"

"That girl the teacher told Vaughan to sit next to didn't look common. Looks as though she's from a good background. The teacher probably sat him there because he looks refined. People can tell."

"He does look refined, doesn't he, Rene?"

"Yes, he does."

"Well, how did you get on, Vaughan? Not too bad, aye?"

"All right."

"I saw they sat you next to that girl. She looked very nice. What is her name?"

"Elizabeth."

She is very nice. I've never sat next to a girl before. The prettiest in the class. And then at the end of school we both walked out to the playground and she got on her bike, waved at me and cycled off – with her dress outside the seat so she must have been sitting on the seat just in her pants! So . . .

"Vaughan. Are you in a dream? You've got to make a go of this, you know. Then you might pass the thirteen plus and go to Skegness Grammar School where Cynthia went. She's training to be a teacher now. Isn't that right, Rene?"

"Yes. Cynthia is doing well."

Cynthia is Auntie Irene's daughter. I look out of the window. We are just passing Butlin's Holiday Camp. There is that big sign again, right across the entrance:

OUR TRUE INTENT IS ALL FOR YOUR DELIGHT!

Father told me it was from Shakespeare. Don't know what Shakespeare has to do with Skegness.

I stayed a year and then begged to come home. Eventually I passed the thirteen plus but didn't go to Skegness Grammar School. Elizabeth did. She was very clever and was transferred at the end of the first term, unfortunately for me. Her dad was an accountant, by the way.

DRIVING TEST OFFICE, NEWARK-ON-TRENT, 1960

*Owning a set of wheels which didn't need pedalling carried status at school.
But only so far as passing your motorcycle riding test. Then you could get
a real bike. I started in the status stakes by buying a 50cc Mobylette moped
with some of my holiday job money.*

"Mr Grylls? I am your Driving Examiner and we are now outside the Ministry of Transport Newark Driving Test Office on Slaughterhouse Lane."

I nod. Of course we are.

"Mr Grylls, I want you to proceed to the end of Slaughterhouse Lane, turn left on to Kings Road, proceed to the junction of Kings Road with Queens Road, turn left on to Queens Road, proceed to the junction of Queens Road with Northgate, turn left on to Northgate and proceed until you see Slaughterhouse Lane on your left, turn left on to Slaughterhouse Lane, returning to where we are now. So it is left, left, left and left. Understood?"

"Er, yes."

"Do you have any questions?"

"Yes. Where will you be?"

"I'll be stepping out into your path at an undisclosed point and holding up my hand like this. When you see me doing this, you must make an Emergency Stop. Do you understand?"

"Er, yes."

"Good. Then off you go, Mr Grylls."

"Your test is now over."

"Have I passed?"

"Leave your motorcycle here, please, and accompany me to the office. Thank you."

I pull out the Mobylette's prop-stand, take off my helmet, straighten up and, trying not to show pain, follow the Examiner through the small entrance towards a door signed "Interview Room".

"Well. Here we are. Sit down please."

I sit without grimacing. (I think.) He sits himself behind the desk.

"Now. Why did you take so long when I sent you off to later perform an Emergency Stop?"

Oh dear. "I was riding slowly . . . and carefully."

"I see. It normally takes candidates about five minutes to cover the circuit I require. You took twelve minutes."

"Did I do the Emergency Stop?"

"Yes, you certainly did. And when I stepped out on Northgate just before you were due to turn left into Slaughterhouse Lane, you were not riding slowly, in my opinion. In fact, if you had carried on at that speed, you may have had difficulty turning the corner at all when it arrived."

"But I did stop all right when you suddenly came out from that passage and held your hand up?"

"Indeed. Indeed."

He looks down at some forms on his desk. Almost as suddenly as when he dashed out of that passage, he leaps up and leans over his desk. I can feel my heart thumping. And the pain.

"Why is your trouser leg torn, Mr Grylls?"

"Oh, that is because they are old school trousers. I did it I think playing football earlier today."

"Really? And you cut your knee earlier today?"

"Er, yes."

"So why is it bleeding now?"

"Er, I don't know. Maybe because I have been moving it. Walking in here."

"Walking in here?"

"Yes."

22

"You fell off your motorcycle, didn't you, Mr Grylls? During your Emergency Stop circuit?"

"But . . ."

"I'm sorry, Mr Grylls. You fell off, hurt your knee and that is why you took so long. I'm going to have to fail you, Mr Grylls. Also for riding too fast for the road conditions on Northgate."

"Well, I am sorry. But it wasn't very much . . ."

He looks me in the eye, down at my knee and back in the eye.

"There is a washbasin in the toilet to the left in the hall. Wash that wound now and get some antiseptic and a bandage on it. You'll find a first aid box above the wash basin. Good day."

I was too embarrassed to return to the Driving Test Office for a couple of years. Eventually I passed my test, but in a car. At least I knew that I would not be examined again by Newark's one and only motorcycle examiner.

MAGNUS GRAMMAR SCHOOL, NEWARK-ON-TRENT, 1961

At school, I always had a problem with teachers who liked humiliating boys.

A music master, Mr Tiffin, favoured putting any boy he disliked into the knee-well of his desk, where he would kick him every now and then. It was Tiffin who pushed my head down on a piano keyboard several times in front of the class after I had announced that I played the piano by ear.

An English master, Mr Todd, was very sarcastic. One of his favourite cruelties was to make a boy stand facing the corner at the front of the class. He would then run at the boy and kick him in the backside while reciting something appropriate such as "To be or not to . . . BE!"

The sad thing was they would always get laughs. So rather than sucking up as many did, with the purpose of becoming a prefect, I decided instead to carry The Secret Sword of Justice, whether these teachers bullied me personally or not. But comeuppance beckoned. Well, nearly.

"Come in, Grylls. Sit down. Grylls, this is Detective Constable Bratby. He would like to ask you a few questions."

Dr Claybourne settles behind his Headmaster's desk and turns to the copper.

"Would you care to take a seat?"

The grim, thin-faced man shakes his head. He pulls out a small black notebook without looking up. That's because he is staring down at me.

"'Ave you been thievin'?"

"No. Why?"

"Well, someone 'as. A birdbath went missin' last week from the front lawn of Dr Dodd's 'ouse. And this week, the column on which it was sat. That boggered off as well."

"Could you please not swear, Detective Constable? This is a grammar school. And, by the way, it is Mr Todd, not Dr Dodd."

"Sorry, Headmaster. Fine by me. I'll make that alteration to the name of the victim of the crime." Detective Constable Bratby fishes in his pocket and produces an india rubber. It then seems like an age for him to erase his mistake. Dr Claybourne is looking irritated. To fill in time, he turns to me.

"Grylls? Have you been to Mr Todd's house at all?"

DC Bratby looks up from his careful erasing. "With due respect, Headmaster, I'll do the interviewin' if you don't mind."

"I'm afraid this is my school and I decide who talks to my pupils while they are here and when. I'm sure you will understand that, Detective Constable. Please remember you came here at my invitation."

I look up at the copper and then at the Headmaster. Could this put Dr Claybourne on my side? I don't think so. His comment is more about him than me.

"Fair enough, Headmaster. Fair enough. But it was your Mr Dodd that complained to the police and it was us who 'ad to ask your permission in 'ere. But let's get on with it, then."

The Headmaster grimaces.

"So. What's your first name, son?"

"Vaughan."

"Vaughan, eh? That's unusual. May I call you by your first name?"

"Yes."

"Good. So . . . 'Ave you nicked a birdbath, Vaughan?"

"Why would I want a concrete birdbath?"

"Ha ha! So why would you know it was concrete?"

Dr Claybourne interjects. "I suppose most of them are."

I seize on this. "Ours is. I cast it from a dustbin lid myself."

The copper pauses. I can press on.

"So I wouldn't need another one, would I?"

The copper's bogus friendly manner evaporates instantly.

"Now then. Don't you start getting clever with me, Sonny Jim. Or we'll 'ave to continue with this interview down the station."

"I'd prefer this to remain in the school for the moment, Detective Constable. The information you have?"

The copper shrugs, looks down at his notebook and starts flicking back a few pages.

"A neighbour of Dr Dale."

"Mr Todd." I interrupt cheekily.

"A neighbour of Mr Todd says he saw two youths, one answering your description – a lot of fair 'air, about five foot ten – 'anging about the night of the first reported crime. The other fits the description of Stephen Smith-Creed. That gentleman, I understand, is a friend of yours?"

"I'd prefer we didn't mention the other pupil at this moment, Detective Constable."

"Sorry, but that is what was told to my Inspector by Mr Dodd." He turns to me. A phoney smile now.

"Well, Vaughan. Was you there?"

"No."

"I see. Well, you won't mind taking part in an identity parade then, will you?"

Now he has got me. I cannot refuse.

"No."

"Is there anything else, Detective Constable?"

"Just one or two things, Headmaster."

"Vaughan. Do you refer to Mr Dodd in a disrespectful way, especially in the presence of younger pupils?"

"I don't understand."

"Vaughan. I think you do understand." He consults his notebook.

"You refer to him in public as 'Cod-Eyes'?"

Do I see a very slight smile play across the Headmaster's lips?

"It is Mr Todd's nickname. Everyone calls him that."

"I see. And everyone puts up a sign on the top of a piano in the school hall saying, er, let me see, 'A Song For Cod-Eyes. Join in at 1pm today.' Did you write that and was you the one playing the piano in the school hall at dinner time to younger pupils leading a chorus of er . . ."

He consults his notebook again.

"'Bye Bye Birdbath, Bye Bye'. Thus producing a humorous atmosphere."

"Er, yes. It was quite humorous . . ."

The Headmaster intervenes again.

"Whether you stole Mr Todd's birdbath or not, Grylls, it was in bad taste and it gave a poor example to younger boys. I'll be dealing with that particular incident, Detective Constable. Do you have any further questions of Grylls?"

"No, sir. That is all we need to know for the moment. We'll be in touch about the identity parade."

Dr Claybourne turns to me.

"That is all, Grylls. I"ll be speaking to you later. As you will not be surprised to hear."

I get up, nod to the Headmaster, nod to the copper and leave. My legs are shaking. I am fucking sunk. Identity parade. I'll be expelled. At the very least.

I'm now standing, next to my Mobylette, outside the Newark Magnus Grammar School and I'm nervously dragging on a fag, which I cover between puffs with my helmet. Oh no. Here is the copper. He is marching in my direction. Here he is. He now has his thin, mean face right in front of mine. The fag is ignored, but the tone is menacing.

"Hullo, Vaughan. Lookin' forward to the identity parade? You won't 'ave to wait long. By the way, was you acquainted with a Dr Tiffin?"

"Mr Tiffin? Oh, yes. He taught music here. I think he went to Yorkshire."

"Indeed he did, Vaughan. Indeed he did. 'Is life was made miserable here. By people like you, Vaughan, weren't it?"

"I didn't know that."

"Oh, you did, Vaughan. Oh, you did. Was you the one responsible for sending 'im some outsize women's corsets from Gamages in London? Cash on delivery?"

I can feel the cigarette burning my fingers inside the helmet. I'm trying to squeeze it out.

"Maybe his wife ordered them?"

"Don't try and be humorous with me, Vaughan. It doesn't suit you.

As you 'ave brought up Mrs Tiffin, was it you who rang up Roses Funeral Directors last year pretending to be another party? Asking them to collect 'er body? They then went round there, didn't they?"

"Oh? I didn't know she had died."

"I'll 'ave you, Vaughan. I'll 'ave you. Take my word for it."

Clapping me on the shoulder, he turns abruptly and walks away.

The identity parade took place. But the neighbour failed to recognise any-body. Which was strange as we had asked him very foolishly where Cod-Eyes lived, after which we did the deed. It was many years before I heard that the neighbour loathed Mr Todd. As for the concrete birdbath, followed by its pedestal a week later, they ended up in the River Trent and they are probably still there.

NOTTINGHAM COLLEGE OF ARTS & CRAFTS, 1963

I applied to Bath Academy of Art for a Pre-Diploma course (today called Foundation Art & Design) but Nottinghamshire Education Authority said that even if I was offered a place there they would not pay the fees as they had a local art college for me to attend where they would pay the fees, assuming I was accepted.

Nottingham College of Arts & Crafts overlooks a cemetery. I can see it from the Principal's office where I am standing wearing Uncle Charles's suit, loaned for the purpose of this very interview. I feel great. I should. My mother says he is a dapper dresser.

The Principal, Robert Scott, and the Head of Pre-Diploma, John Powell, are staring at my pictures on the floor.

"They all have the same number of figures in them, more or less. Why?"

"Mr White says we should always have at least three figures in our pictures but not more than six. He's our art teacher."

"I see. These titles on bits of paper – *A Day at the Seaside, The Engineers, A Windy Day* – why do you clip them to each painting?"

"So I know which one I've done. We have a list of titles to choose from in the art room. When you've finished one, you have to start another."

"Oh? Okay."

The Head of Pre-Diploma pulls out two more.

"Do you own a portfolio?"

"No. Just this suitcase. It belongs to my Uncle Charles. He took it to

San Remo and back. San Remo . . . it's in Italy."

"Yes, quite."

Two more are pulled out.

"These are not too bad."

He is now looking backwards and forwards at *The Funfair* in one hand and *In the Wings at the Theatre* in the other. Off they go to join the others on the floor.

"Do you mind if I . . .?"

"No. Please take out whatever you would like to see."

He rummages in the suitcase. Out comes a book.

"Erasmus of Rotterdam?"

"Pottery Prize, 1961. It is properly inscribed on the inside cover."

"Indeed."

More rummaging. Uncle Charles's suitcase has become a bran tub.

"Do you have your pottery in this . . . shoebox?"

"No, that is for my sculptures – made by melting plastic pens on the kitchen stove. It's not schoolwork."

"Okay. And this? *In Lordly Style?*"

He flicks open the pages of a home-made book he has now discovered. So embarrassing. Why did I bring that? Fuck.

"My brother David and I made it about how people should dress and speak in England. It's in three sections – Upper Class, Middle Class and Lower Class. I did most of the drawings, my brother David did most of the writing. He is younger than me. Three years younger. Perhaps that will help explain its . . . er . . .?"

"I want to sit in the back of a Rolls Royce and ignore guttersnipes?"

Silence. The Principal breaks in.

"May we take a look at your sculptures?"

I nod and open the shoebox.

"Please. Lay them out here. On my desk."

I do as I'm told and then take the titles written on bits of cardboard out of the bottom of the box and place one under each. I think I can remember the right order.

The Head of Pre-Diploma stares in close.

"Mr Clarke, Mr Bannister, Dr Claybourne . . .?"

"They're the names of my teachers at various schools. This one is of the Head of the Southwell Minster Choir School. This one of Skegness Secondary Modern. This one, Doctor Claybourne, is the Headmaster of Newark Magnus Grammar School. I went to seven different schools."

The Head of Pre-Diploma returns to examining *In Lordly Style*. More silence. It is his turn to break it.

"Maybe you need a period focused on developing a greater degree of maturity. We do evening classes in life drawing and you . . ."

The Principal breaks in.

"But Mr Grylls lives in Newark. It would be a long way for him to go. Twenty miles, is it?"

I nod. More excruciating silence. I'm sure they will see the sweat pouring through my new *Elegante Signor* shirt.

"I think Mr Grylls has some potential. A quirkiness? Well, would you like him on our Pre-Diploma course?"

The Head of Pre-Diploma looks up from *In Lordly Style*. He nods. Sulkily.

I was offered a place and stayed the year, at the end of which I applied to half a dozen art schools for their Diploma in Art & Design courses. I was eventually taken on by Walsall. They were desperate to fill places.

LEICESTER COLLEGE OF ART, 1964

In 1964, Leicester College of Art was the largest and most prestigious art school outside London. I had applied from Nottingham but I didn't even get an interview. So after a few weeks at Walsall I decided to take the bull by the horns by writing to the Head of Sculpture at Leicester, Albert Carstairs, to ask him to interview me. I did not think for a moment that I would even get a reply, so I was totally gobsmacked when Mr Carstairs wrote back to say "Come along."

"Thank you agreeing to look at my portfolio and give me advice, Mr Carstairs."

"That's okay."

He leafs through my portfolio laid out on his desk.

Say it now. While he is looking at your work.

"I want to leave Walsall College of Art and come here."

Without looking up. "Really? So, tell me, Vaughan – it is Vaughan isn't it? – why exactly do you want to leave Walsall?"

"Well, I think it is . . . provincial."

"Provincial. Well, I suppose Walsall is in the provinces, but so is Leicester. Is that it?"

"Well . . . er . . . no. It's more. It's because, it's because . . . I don't honestly believe I could get into anywhere good from there."

"Such as where?"

"The Slade or the Royal College of Art? Or the Royal Academy Schools?"

Mr Carstairs closes the portfolio on his desk and, without glancing at me, walks over to the window and stares out. In the background, a drill whines away in a workshop somewhere. "Somebody is busy," he says.

I'll have to have another go.

"The thing is that, well, how shall I say this? Well, the fine art students on my course at Walsall are there, like me, because they couldn't get in anywhere else. And this has been an awful shock to me. Because I had thought I was the only one who couldn't get in anywhere else. Anyway, as I hope you can see, I've managed to do some sculpture. And drawing. I've worked hard. Against the odds. But the other thing is . . . about half of the students in fine arts had applied to do painting and they are only doing sculpture because the Government turned down the college for teaching painting. They aren't really sculpture students at all. They are painting students having to pretend to be sculpture students. At least I applied to do sculpture. The whole thing is, well, ridiculous . . . and upsetting."

Mr Carstairs turns from looking out of the window and, still avoiding my gaze, returns to his desk. He sits, staring into space before getting up and going to stare out of the window again. Then,

"Do you know Wallows Lane?"

"Wallows Lane? In Walsall?"

"Yes, Vaughan."

"It is near Fellows Park. The football ground."

"So it is. My mother lives there. She's getting on a bit now."

She must be. He's getting on a bit himself. But what has this got to do with . . . oh no.

"I think your problem is you are a bit of a snob."

"Well, I don't . . ."

"Why are you interested, Vaughan, in how good or bad other students are? Just concentrate on your own work. You've got the makings of some good stuff there. If you really want to, you can transfer here, but my strong advice to you is to stay where you are, because Walsall has an historic reputation for sculpture. However, it is entirely up to you."

He returns to his desk, ties my portfolio up and slides it towards me. He now looks me straight in the eye.

"Well?"

"Er, I'll carry on at Walsall."

"Good decision."

I pick up my portfolio and back out for the door. He runs behind and opens it while extending his hand.

It is then I say, "Did you like being a student at Walsall College of Art?"

"Yes. They did very well for this Black Country boy."

The door closes behind me. On the outside:

> "Head of Sculpture
> Albert Carstairs ARCA"

Associate of the Royal College of Art. Thus does this silly snob wend his weary way back to the Black Country.

I never returned to Leicester College of Art. Even now I cringe when I recall this interview.

GOLDSMITHS SCHOOL OF ART, 1967

Goldsmiths had the best postgraduate art and design teacher-training course in the country. It was heavily oversubscribed as the course demanded that students continue with their own art or design work alongside learning to teach schoolchildren. Indeed, part of the examination was on the artwork students had produced during their year on the course. Many years later, when I was in a position to do so, I shamelessly copied the course by opening an additional one at West Hall. But that was in 1978 and here we are in 1967.

There are two of us sitting in a narrow corridor waiting to be called. One has to break the awful silence. It will have to be me.

"Hello. Not much room in here, is there? Is that your portfolio?"

"Yeah. Course."

I gaze out of the window of this little house in Laurie Grove, New Cross. I can see Goldsmiths College a road away. It is a big redbrick building.

"I suppose this house is owned by Goldsmiths."

"Yeah, suppose so."

"I'm Vaughan. You?"

"Nigel."

"I'm from the art college in Walsall."

"Huh. Walsall to Goldsmiths?"

I'll counter that.

"So which college are *you* from, Nige?"

"It's Nigel. Goldsmiths."

"Okay. So, er . . . what are you doing here . . . if you are here already I mean?

"Well, this is a postgraduate interview, isn't it?"

"Yes, but it is only the Art Teachers Certificate course."

Nigel shrugs.

"You could say that. More than three hundred applicants for thirty places."

"Oh. I see."

Silence. I"ll try again.

"I suppose it's because it is the only postgrad teacher training course in an art school where you can carry on as an artist."

"Of course. That's why you applied, didn't you . . . from Walsall?"

Ignore this mockery and gaze out the window. Let Nige return to examining his shoes. He is not going to rattle me.

"One of the interviewers is famous, you know."

"Oh? What for?"

"For not taking prisoners."

"Prisoners?"

"At interviews. He can be a right bastard at interviews."

"Oh. What is his name?"

"Dr Anton Ehrensweig. He teaches on the course you are applying for. He is an expert on art and psychology. An Austrian. You must have heard of his books?"

Don't reply, Vaughan. Just wait and hold that name in your head. Nige will return to examining his shoes. Now, fish in your pockets for a pen and scribble that name on your palm. Look at it. Repeat it. Silently. The bastard.

A door opens. Nige looks up. A girl emerges, portfolio under arm. She hurries past like the White Rabbit, nodding at Nige and ignoring me.

"Is she on your course?"

"Yeah."

"Do you think she will get in?"

"No. Might get into Hornsey. Not so many apply there. She didn't get into the Slade postgrad. No way was she going to get in there."

I don't like these glum remarks. I'm going to say something.

"Well, you never know. She might get in here and you might have to go to Hornsey!"

He looks up and stares at me. It is the first time I've seen him look alive.

"Hey. Cool it, man. Okay?"

The door opens.

"Vaughan Grylls?"

"Hello. I'm Arnold Keefe. This is Anton Ehrensweig. Now, could you just, er, spread some of your work from your portfolio on the floor?"

Here.

Undo the portfolio. Take out some life drawings and half a dozen photos of my sculptures.

"Thanks so much. Take a seat. So, why do you want to teach?"

"Well, I admired my art teachers at school."

"Oh, why was that?"

"Because, unlike the other teachers, they didn't have to mark any homework."

Glances exchanged.

"I'm . . . only joking [first lie]. Sorry [second lie]. I admired the way they encouraged creativity in children [third lie]."

"And how did they do that?"

"Well, at my last school we had to do pictures with four or five figures in them for the GCE . . . but the art teacher also didn't mind when I brought in little abstract sculptures of the teachers . . . made out of melted pens. He put them up . . . in the art room. And I then put titles underneath on little labels – the name of each teacher, that is. A lot of people were amused by that, including even him – well, a bit. He wasn't a person with much of a sense of humour. He was a potter, you see."

"Well, I suppose ceramicists aren't necessarily known for their sense of humour."

I've said too much. Mr Keefe points to the portfolio.

"Do you have any photos of those works?"

"No. They were thrown away long ago. Just these I've done at Walsall. And some life drawings from beforehand . From art college in Nottingham."

"Well. Let us take a look."

"This life drawing was done in 1964. When I was at Nottingham."

"We can see."

"Oh?"

"You've written 'Life Drawing V. F. Grylls Nottingham 1964' in the top right-hand corner."

"Oh, yes. So I have. Well. Here are photos of a sculpture I made in Walsall in 1966. In fibreglass."

"A big yellow, uprooted tree. Life size?"

"Yes. It's the largest sculpture I have ever made."

I glance up at Mr Keefe who has done all the talking. Mr Ehrensweig has not asked one question so far. It is unlikely he will as he appears to have fallen asleep. This is a disaster.

"It's called *Wimpey Tree*. Painted Wimpey yellow. They were uprooting trees outside Walsall to build posh houses . . . called, er, executive homes. Here's another photo of it. Taken by the *Walsall Evening Post.*"

"Black-and-white press photo. So some of the point is lost for the reader . . . the title, the colour?"

"Yes, I suppose so. But it is in a different context now."

"In a car park . It is in a car park, isn't it? Or do you mean in a newspaper?"

"Both. It now has a new title, you see. 'A Peculiar Piece of Sculpture Had Car Park Attendant Guessing.' The *Walsall Evening Post* came up with that."

"H'mm. And the children looking at it?"

"I rang up a primary school which was nearby and asked if they would like to bring some of their pupils down to see a tree parked in a car park."

"How did you introduce it? To the school."

"Er, I said that you can always see cars parked next to trees but not trees parked next to cars."

"Huh."

God. What else can I show Mr Keefe. Here we go. Nothing to lose? Is Mr Ehrensweig now snoring?

The Drunken Clergyman. What's in a Name. A Day at the Seaside. Out they come. One by one. And on I babble.

"So . . . What other interests can you point to that inform your sculptures?"

"Um, actually I am quite interested in er, linguistic philosophy. And in . . . Ludwig Wittgenstein!"

A triumph of foolishness. But who cares? I know fuck-all about linguistic philosophy and Ludwig Wittgenstein, apart from the fact that he furnished his house with deck chairs.

"Wittgenstein! Wittgenstein!"

Ehrensweig has woken up. Maybe they were drinking mates in Vienna.

He gesticulates at the photographs on the floor.

"*The Drunken Clergyman. What's in a Name?* The titles of your sculptures appear to be integral to the sculptures themselves, although they are not physically present in the work. Have you explored the philosophical implications of that?"

Now. Go for it, Vaughan.

"A bit. But not in words. The main weakness of linguistic philosophy in my view is that it is trying to study words whilst using them. That's why I investigate in sculpture. Such things I plan to research more deeply should I be offered a place at Goldsmiths!"

As I won't be offered a place at Goldsmiths it is okay to say what I like, including that genius bullshit reply.

I spent the best year of my life at Goldsmiths. As for the linguistic investigation, I confined it to projects for schoolchildren such as getting them to make contorted drawings and sculptures on topics such as "Foot in Mouth". I also helped set up a street theatre group called Further Granulated Advice which we named by selecting three random words from a newspaper.

THE SLADE SCHOOL OF FINE ART, 1968

In 1968, while still on the teacher-training course at Goldsmiths, I applied for the postgraduate course at the Slade School of Fine Art, which is the Art Department of University College, London. It is a very small school – about two hundred students – and, as perhaps the most prestigious Fine Art school in the world, is almost impossible to get a place at. But my girl-friend at the time, sadly soon to be ex-girlfriend, persuaded me to apply. I thought I had no chance so I was thunderstruck when I was called for in-terview at such a formidably illustrious establishment.

I swing my 1956 VW Beetle, registration number RTR 301, with its mi-nuscule rear window, through the main entrance of University College London on Gower Street because I have a new, wooden portfolio made by myself no less. It is the only way I can get the heavy beast here so now I will have to explain all this to those two top-hatted beadles guarding the en-trance, one of whom is now walking towards the driver's door.

"Good morning, sir. How may we help you?"

"I have an interview at your Slade School of Fine Art. In sculpture. And my portfolio is heavy. It is on the back seat."

"Ah yes. So you have your sculpture in that box?"

"No, it is empty."

"Empty sir?"

"Well, they took the work out when I applied, so the Slade has it. But they asked me to collect the box from the submission centre next to the National Gallery. They didn't want it. So I"ll put my work back in this box after my interview."

"Really, sir. We were not informed you would be arriving by car and expecting to park."

"I'm very sorry. But my interview for Sculpture is in ten minutes. Very sorry. Please. Look."

I push the letter inviting me for interview out of the driver's window. He takes the letter and scrutinises it.

"Well, sir. You had better park over there, in front of the Slade. I will give you an hour. No longer, please."

"Much appreciated. Very much."

I park, drag said portfolio off the back seat and up the steps as quickly as I can. God, it is heavy. Why did I make this ridiculous thing? Luckily another beadle must have seen my struggles through the window for he emerges on cue to hold open the sacred entrance door.

"Good morning, sir. Interview?"

"Yes."

"Would you have your letter of invitation with you, sir?"

"Yes, yes! Here it is."

"Thank you. H'mm. Well, according to this, you have your interview in five minutes. So you had better get your skates on, sir!"

"Yes, I know!"

"Now sir, if you turn right and descend the stairs over there you will reach a corridor. Turn left and you will see a chair opposite a room on the right. You will need to wait there."

God. Down here. Down there. There it is. Collapse into chair. I've made it. Just. Sir indeed. In an art school.

And then the wait. Fifteen minutes it must be until the door opposite swings open.

"Grylls? Mr Vaughan Grylls? Hello. I'm Dick Claughton. Thank you so much for coming."

"Vaughan Grylls. May I introduce you to Reg Butler and Philip King."

They already have the photographs of my sculptures spread out on the floor.

Hands shaken. Reg Butler and Philip King look almost identical, apart from the fact that Reg Butler is older than Philip King and is wearing red socks. Both wear cavalry twill trousers and cavalry twill colour jumpers. Dick Claughton is in a tweed jacket and tie. He is smoking a pipe.

All three are quietly polite and speak in posh accents. This is quite terrifying – nothing like Goldsmiths and certainly not Nottingham or Birmingham or Coventry or Walsall art schools. Relaxed, unhurried, intimidating.

What does all this remind me of. Of course – that interview at St Paul's Cathedral Choir School, aged seven.

"This visual–verbal stuff is quite interesting, Grylls," muses Reg Butler.

Then Philip King. He gestures towards my photos of *Ku Klux Klan, The Drunken Clergyman, Wimpey Tree* and *A Day at the Seaside*

"I say. Could you say something about these sculptures? Do take your time."

When I reach the last one, Reg Butler interjects, "Well. Quite droll."

Back to Philip King. "What are you doing now?"

"I'm just on the Art Teachers' Certificate course at Goldsmiths."

Feel a bit embarrassed about that.

"Yes, I didn't quite mean that. Are you managing to continue making sculpture? Do you find time?"

"I try. It means working at the Hammersmith Evening Institute in Lime Grove. I'm afraid the work I do there is very modest, though – actually it's a bit sad after the stuff I used to make, but that's because I don't have the time and space I had at Walsall. Just these two - *Old Jewry* and *HQ*."

"H'mmm, yes. Have you done anything else other than these since leaving art school at Walsall?"

"I've just had an exhibition in the Underground."

"Oh?"

"Well, last summer, I had a job in Accrington in Lancashire, where my ex- girlfriend is from, in the drawing office of a gas fire company. I designed two of their new gas fire badges."

Reg Butler fixes me. "And the connection with the Underground?"

"Oh yes. Well, last week, I was standing waiting for a train in an Underground station when I saw a big poster opposite for a new gas fire and my badge was on it. About six inches wide! And I've since seen it in other Underground stations."

Dick Claughton takes out his pipe to have a quiet chuckle. Philip King smiles wanly. Reg Butler is impassive. He is now peering at my application form.

"Where are you living now? Newark? That's up in Nottinghamshire isn't it? How is it you're at Goldsmiths?"

"I've just broken up with my girlfriend and I'm between living in my old place in Battersea with her and a new place in Lewisham I hope to move into next week, so I suppose my address is RTR 301."

"What?" says Reg Butler. "What's that?"

"That's the number-plate of my car. It's a Beetle. It's parked outside right now."

"Well," says Reg Butler, "I don't think we have any more questions. Do you have any for us?"

"No, thank you, but thank you for bothering to see me."

I start packing up my work. Reg Butler then says, "Well, thank you so much for coming and showing us your work and talking about it. Impressive portfolio."

Everyone nods. Polite smiles all round. I am taken aback.

"Any work in particular?"

"No, no, I mean that splendid box you've made. It's clearly built to last a lifetime!"

I drag the splendid box into RTR 301. Drive out and down Gower Street.

I was offered a Sculpture place at the Slade, one of five out of over three hundred applicants. Amazing.

UNDERGRADUATE TOURS LTD, 1969

In early June 1969, at the end of my first year at the Slade, I saw an advertisement pinned up on the main student notice board at University College London for summer jobs with a company called Undergraduate Tours Ltd. They were looking for guides – "Applications are particularly welcome from public school-educated and/or Oxford/Cambridge undergraduates." I took it down so no one else would see it. Then I rang them for an interview (poshest accent on the phone, explain I'm a postgraduate at the Slade, not just an undergraduate) and when they said come in this afternoon, I put on my only suit and made for their office which was one small room up a narrow flight of stairs in London's South Molton Street.

"Fantastic, Vaughan. Could you wait here a mo? We'll see you guys one at a time and then take a drive."

He pops back into the room, leaving me sitting in a narrow corridor next to Toby (cravat, blazer) and Simon (suit, tie, yellow socks).

Toby lets it be known he is at Oxford and he is also "an Honourable."

"Not that I use it, of course."

"Of course," says Simon. "I'm afraid I'm merely at Cambridge." adding, "Rugby and Cambridge."

My turn.

"I'm afraid I am dishonourably at the Slade."

Quizzical smiles.

Toby is called in first, followed by Simon. Only ten minutes each. Maybe less.

Now me.

In the tiny interview room stacked with piles of papers, brochures, typewriters and two telephones, sit the man who invited me and a woman. Both are in their late twenties and both have public school accents. So that is everyone around here except me. Get in first, Vaughan.

"I have not gone to a public school, although I've been to every other school going. And I'm not at Oxford or Cambridge."

"Yah, but you are a postgraduate at the Slade."

"Yes."

"So where have you been educated other than there?"

"Well, educated may be too grand a description. I think I'm self-educated.

"An auto-didact? Tell us more. This sounds interesting." The woman interviewer has got it.

"I started at Highfields Preparatory School in Newark-on-Trent – that was quite posh – and then I got into St Paul's Choir School, although I was thrown out for wetting the bed, but I was only eight you know, then I was sent to Southwell Minster Choir School as it was down the road and it didn't matter if I wet the bed as I went home at night, and there I failed the eleven plus, and then I went to Skegness Secondary Modern School, Newark Parish Secondary Modern School, Newark Magnus Grammar School – I passed the thirteen plus but hated it there, so pretentious, trying to be like a public school, and then Nottingham College of Art."

"I say, old chap, how many more places? I'm losing track already!" says he.

"Nearly there. Walsall College of Art, Goldsmiths College of Art . . ."

"And now the Slade?" says she.

"Yes."

"You could write a book on education."

"Or lack of it!"

"Huh. We do specialise in educated clients staying at the best hotels, who are looking for a personalised tour with an educated and knowledge-able guide. And a charming one. That goes without saying, of course. They are looking for a morning or an afternoon tour of London. Or an all-day outing to places like Oxford. Sometimes a couple of days away. That may be, say, ancestor hunting. You'd have to think on your feet. Usually we have Americans but not always. Japanese have money and curiosity. Can you think of a one-day tour and what you would call it?"

My brain is racing. Let me think . . . what is it called? I went with Mother last year . . . Yes, Bladon, near Oxford.

"Er, 'Graves of the Two Greatest Englishmen'?"

"What?"

"Just something to hang a tour to Oxford and Stratford-on-Avon on – with a run through the Cotswolds in between. You know. Churchill and Shakespeare?"

"I see, yes. It's a good idea," says the man. "But for Americans, maybe 'Resting Places of the Two Greatest Englishmen'."

"What about in London?" says the woman.

"Westminster Abbey, St Paul's. Maybe one or the other if short of time. And the Changing of the Guard at Buckingham Palace. And maybe where the Virginia Company started? Americans would like that. And an old pub. The Cheshire Cheese? And . . . er . . . something more thought-provoking . . . I know . . . the grave of Karl Marx in Highgate."

"You seem to like graves."

"Well, you can tell stories there. John Wesley's grave in Bunhill Fields. Americans are religious and a lot are nonconformists, aren't they?"

"Okay. Good. So. What car do you have, how old is it and are you insured?"

"A VW Beetle. 1964. Very immaculate. My mother bought it for my brother and he will lend it to me as he doesn't need it over the summer. And I'm insured."

"A Beetle. I see. Could take two clients. Three at a push." says she.

"One American or four Japanese?"

God, I shouldn't have said that but just couldn't resist. Now my interviewers are turning to look at one another. She turns back to me.

"Vaughan, would you pop out of the room for a moment?"

"We'd like all three of you to take our knowledge of London test. We'll be driving you round for half an hour. And we'll be pointing things out, asking you to talk about them briefly. Okay? We'll get the car."

A Humber Hawk draws up outside Undergraduate Tours and out

hops the same man – one of our interviewers and now the driver and our examiner. Toby and Simon are waved to the back seat, me to the front.

"You'll be taking it in turns. I"ll point something out and you can then tell me what you know about it. You first, Vaughan."

"Harrods. London's leading department store. Used by royalty."

"Good, Vaughan. Point out the Royal Coats of Arms outside. Okay?"

"Simon?"

"Sloane Square. Royal Court Theatre over there."

"And?"

"Er, 'kitchen sink' plays first performed there. *Look Back in Anger* etc."

"You'll either have to explain kitchen sink or don't mention that bit. Remember, you are driving and you'll be on to the next."

"Toby?"

"Er, oh yes. Marble Arch?"

"No, Toby. This is Hyde Park Corner. Marble Arch is at the north end of Park Lane."

"Oh gosh! Sorry!"

For the next twenty minutes Simon and I get nearly everything right, poor old Toby nearly everything wrong.

Back to Undergraduate Tours.

"Could you all come in please?"

There are five of us now squeezed into the tiny office that is Undergraduate Tours.

"Well, I'm pleased to say you have all passed. Toby, you need to do a bit of brushing up. Now you will each have a card printed which we will arrange. Yours, Vaughan, will say, 'Vaughan Grylls, Graduate Student, Slade School, University College London'. Yours, Simon, 'Simon Gulliver, Trinity College, University of Cambridge'. Yours, Toby, The Hon. Toby Whittingstall-Stanley, St Peter's College, University Of Oxford'."

The woman now looks down at her notes.

"Now, you, Simon have your father's Wolseley, you, Toby, your own Jaguar and you, Vaughan, your brother's Beetle. This means you, Simon, can charge seven pounds for a half-day tour, you, Toby, nine pounds and you, Vaughan, five pounds. And fifty per cent of your fee goes to Undergraduate Tours. And you tip the hotel concierge five shillings from your share for each tour he books with you. Any questions?"

"Gosh, that sounds generous! What do we wear?"

"A dark suit and tie or a cravat and blazer as you are wearing at the moment, Toby. And, Vaughan, I'm afraid either the sideburns or the long hair goes. Your choice."

This is unfair. Toby's hair is longer and scruffier than mine. *And* he has sideburns.

I did this summer job for Undergraduate Tours for nearly two months. It was great. Even without sideburns.

MAIDSTONE COLLEGE OF ART, 1970

Some of the new art and design degree course colleges – Maidstone, for example – would contact postgraduate centres such as the Royal College of Art and the Slade to ask whether they had any student they could recommend to undertake some visiting teaching. It was a way of looking for possible future staff directly from the very few postgraduate centres at a time of expansion across the art and design sector. It was also a way of giving existing staff some time off in the week.

"Either of you interested? One day a week. Maidstone?"

Dick Claughton waves a letter in the Slade's sculpture department. There are only two of us in Sculpture this afternoon.

"Yes, well I would be . . . unless Penny . . ."

Penny shakes her head. "You do it, Vaughan. I'm too busy."

"Good. So, Vaughan, could you get down there tomorrow? For an interview? Midday?"

Maidstone College of Art is in a spanking new building in Oakwood Park. All concrete.

"Hello. I'm Vaughan Grylls for an interview to teach Sculpture. Nice new building."

"Oh hello. You'll be seeing Joe Plant, the Head of Sculpture. It's only just been opened, you know. By Sir Kenneth Clark, no less. He came down from Saltwood Castle to do it. Near Folkestone it is. Doesn't live far away, you see. So he could do it."

"I see."

"You know. He's on the telly. *Civilisation.*"

"Oh, yes. All about civilisation. On the telly. So where do I meet the Head of Sculpture?"

"Joe? Here. He said he would come and collect you here from reception when I let him know you've arrived. I"ll ring him now. Excuse me."

"Let's go to the pub," says Joe.

"I've contacted the Royal Academy Schools, the Royal College of Art, the Slade and I'm hoping to get a postgraduate student teaching in Sculpture every week. It will help us out. Another one?"

"Okay. Thanks."

Joe heads for the bar and then the juke box.

"You like *Sugar Sugar?* The Archies?"

"Er, yes. I suppose so."

"Good. Well, here it comes, Vaughan."

The Archies then come twice more.

> *Sugar, oh, honey, honey*
> *You are my candy girl*
> *And you got me wanting you*
> *Honey, oh, sugar, sugar*
> *You are my candy girl*
> *And you got me wanting you....*

In spite of The Archies, the mood turns sombre.

"The thing is, Vaughan, the ratio between staff and students is going to zoom up at Maidstone. I don't know how we are going to cope."

"Oh, dear. When will all that happen?"

"Next September. So as we're now in May, bringing in postgraduate students to help us teaching the students will give them teaching experience and also help us."

"I see. Sounds like a good plan, Joe. And thank you for interviewing me. Would you like to see some of my work? I've got some photos here."

"Later."

"Why do you like The Archies and *Sugar Sugar?*"

"They are a gas, Vaughan. Don't you think so?"

"Well, hadn't thought of them like that. But what is the staff to student ratio going to be next autumn?"

"Five to one, Vaughan! Up from four to one."

"What would you like me to do – if I get the job?"

"You've got the job, Vaughan. Don't worry about that. Cheers!"

"Cheers! Thank you!"

"You are welcome! Just come in on Fridays. Talk to the students. Don't worry. There won't be many there. You know. Look at their work. Show them yours, but only if you want to."

"Will you be there?"

"Oh, no. I don't come in on Fridays."

"Oh, okay. So, er . . . who does come in, then?"

"Nobody."

"Oh, okay. So, er . . . who will be running the Sculpture department on Fridays?"

"You will, Vaughan! You will! Just make sure there is no trouble. Okay? Another?"

I stayed until the end of that academic year but decided to move on. It was my first art school job. I shall always thank Joe for it.

On one occasion, the day after I had been on an anti-University of London march (I cannot remember what that was about), several students burst into the Sculpture office at lunchtime where I was sitting contemplating my pay slip. They said they were fed up with Maidstone College of Art and wanted me to hand over their academic files. Thinking more quickly than I was accustomed to, I had to make something up. The answer was literally to hand. I would if I could but I couldn't as they were . . . the property of Kent Education Department and they were all kept at the County Hall in Maidstone. I tried to make sure they didn't see I had filched that idea from my pay slip. Poacher turned gamekeeper.

FALMOUTH SCHOOL OF ART, 1970

Falmouth, then as now, was a well-respected art school. The only problem was that it was a hell of a long way from London where most young artists wanted to live. But young artists still have to live, and at a time when nobody bought young artists' work very much, the best thing to do was to get a part-time teaching job in the sort of place you had just graduated from.

It is very welcoming to be met at the station after such a journey by Mrs Withers who says she is the Principal's secretary.

"How did you know it was me?"

"You were the only passenger carrying a portfolio."

"Oh. Isn't anybody else coming down from London for interview?" (Gosh! I may be in with a chance as the only candidate!)

"No. We have another candidate from London. He has already arrived. He is at the Royal College of Art. You may know him. You are at the Slade, aren't you?"

"Yes . . . just. I'm about to graduate, so . . . ."

"Yes, so is he. I have my car outside. We'll go to the Rambler Guest House. We usually use it. I think you will find it very reasonable. He is also staying there, by the way."

Now at the Rambler. I will have to stay in my room. No rambling. Then I just might may avoid the other candidate. "He" is bound to be one of those sculpture students I embarrassingly lectured on my visit to the RCA two months ago. On what constituted cutting edge art (mine), and what didn't (theirs).

Following morning, starving, I no longer care. I will not forgo break-fast.

"Hullo, Vaughan. It's Malcolm. Remember me? Here for the same thing?"

"Breakfast?"

"No, the interview, Vaughan. Given any good lectures lately? Mind if I join you? Pass the toast, will you? Ta."

"Just the two of us then. Up for a two-day a week job."

"No, Vaughan. There are two more candidates. One teaching at Bristol, the other Cardiff Art School, I think. That's what they said yesterday when I went over to have a look around. Meet people. You know."

"Oh. You've been around? "

"Yeah. Meet some staff and students. You know. Like you thought of when you came into our Sculpture School earlier this year. To tell us about your sculpture. Ha Ha."

This is appalling.

He stands. Quickly. "Well. Need to get going. We're being picked up in half an hour."

Finish your toast. Stay seated. Look up. Speak slowly.

"I've been doing some teaching, Malcolm. At Maidstone College of Art."

"Oh yeah? I think that was one I turned down. I've done a bit of visiting lecturing – down here actually . . . not that it means anything. I may have pissed them off already! See yah in a bit, Vaughan."

There are four of us outside the interview room. All men.

"Mr Grylls? I'm Robert Jackson, Registrar. Will you please come in?"

I am shocked. There must be at least twenty of them sitting around in a semi-circle at one end of the interview room.

"Hello, Mr Grylls. I'm Lady Donaldson, Chair of Governors. I'm afraid the Principal cannot be here today, so you will have to settle for me. Thank you so much for coming. Did you have a good journey here? All the way down from Paddington. Quite a hike, isn't it? Do take a seat."

"Yes, thank you. Yes, it is."

Her Ladyship is seated in the centre of this orchestra, looking and sounding like Lady Barnet in *Animal, Vegetable or Mineral* on the telly.

"Good. Good. Splendid."

"Now, we've all had a chance to take a peek at your portfolio, and . . ." – here she waves a sheet of paper – "your reference from Sir William Coldstream. So now we are going to take a peek at you . . . and you at us!"

I scan the sea of faces. Two students? Three lecturers? The rest governors probably. Two women wearing hats. Three men wearing waistcoats. The one at the end on the right could be Mr Pickwick.

"And the way we are going to do this is to take it in turns. And when we have asked you our questions, it will be your turn to ask me questions. If you have any, of course. And I'll do my very best to answer them. What does that sound like?"

"Yes, fine."

"Good. Now. So let us start on my extreme left. Councillor Pickwick?"

He leans back. This is his moment. The buttons on his waistcoat are about to pop.

"Mr Grylls. What do you think of that Henry Moore? Bit too clever for you? Or maybe a bit too old-fashioned, eh? Be honest."

"Well. He is probably clever. And gifted. But I suppose times move on."

"And if you are employed here, you"ll move them on . . eh?"

"Well, I"ll try and teach old approaches alongside new ones."

"Like your . . . pun-sculpture, eh?"

"Well, I . . ."

Her Ladyship rides to the rescue.

"I think that is an interesting answer from Mr Grylls. Mr Garbutt. Your turn."

"Mr Grylls. Do you think having girl students is a good idea in sculpture? Are they strong enough to study it properly? All these big things now being expected. You know."

"Yes, I do. Barbara Hepworth makes big things down here in Cornwall – as you know. And Elisabeth Frink . . . and . . ."

"Yes, I know about Miss Hepworth. But she has a lot of assistants, doesn't she?"

"Does she?"

Garbutt nods. "I know she does."

"Well, let us move on. To our first student representative. Mr – ?"

"David. Ainsworth."

"Ah yes. Mr Ainsworth."

"Vaughan. Would you let students work in painting and sculpture at the same time? You know. We need to break down barriers. Just one Fine Art. No painting. No sculpture."

Twenty pairs of eyes scan me. Including presumably those of the Head of Painting and the Head of Sculpture.

"Well, I don't know enough, you know, about . . ."

Her Ladyship to the rescue. "This post is purely teaching sculpture two days a week. I think that is a question of policy . . . for the academic board."

David Ainsworth glares at her Ladyship. Now I can see who the heads of painting and sculpture are for they are now glaring at him.

"Do you think Pop Art is wonderful and, more importantly, Mr Grylls, would you regard yourself as a Pop Artist?"

On and on the questions go . . . all on their own . . . none related to one another.

"Well, Mr Grylls. This has been most interesting. We've been delving away. Now it is your turn. What would you like to know?"

"Er, do you meet travelling expenses for part-time lecturers?"

A pause. She glances down at my application form.

"I see you live in London, Mr Grylls."

I nod.

"Mr Grylls. We do pay weekly travelling expenses for this post . . . but only, I'm afraid, from the Cornish border."

"Oh! Christ!"

Now outside the interview room. Got to have a shit. That is it, then. Cost more to get here than I'm getting paid. That's if I'm offered the job. Not that I will be. Did I actually say "Oh Christ"? Well, bollocks to it. Just sit here having a shit. No hurry while the last candidate is in. Maybe they will think I'm so great they will pay travelling expenses all the way from London? Will they? Don't be stupid, Vaughan. You've just put yourself in the shit and now you're having one.

A door opens. A booming, male voice.

"Mr Grylls? Are you in here? It's Robert Jackson, Registrar."

"Oh yes? I'll be out shortly."

"No hurry, Mr Grylls. I'm afraid we have offered the position to another candidate. Thank you so much for coming. And please don't forget to submit your travel expenses on the form we provided. From London. Thank you."

The candidate who got the job? You are right.

UNIVERSITY OF READING, 1970

I was so desperate to get a part-time teaching job in an art school that I applied for one teaching plastic vacuum forming two days a week at Reading. I did not have a clue about plastic vacuum forming, so I went to see the Slade Professor, Sir William Coldstream, to ask for his help.

The Slade Professor makes two phone calls, one to a Professor Misha Black, Head of Industrial Design at the Royal College of Art. "It is the sort of thing Misha will know about. Go down there and they will find someone to teach you, dear."

The other is to Professor Claude Rogers, Head of Fine Art at the University of Reading. I don't know what he says to him as I am waved out of the room when he is put through. Anyway, now I have been called for interview and I also have a week's industrial experience at the Royal College of Art. I will be able to wax lyrical about plastic vacuum forming.

Exit train at Reading and start psyching myself up as I'm walking through a park with a big, black, flat lion in the middle of it.

"Mr Grylls? You found us. Good journey? Would you be so kind as to take a seat here? Sorry it is just a corridor. I'll inform Professor Rogers you have arrived."

No other candidates? Maybe nobody fancies plastic vacuum forming. Just me. Anyway, I desperately need a job and, Vaughan, you'll be able to wax lyrical about plastic vacuum forming. So *don't worry*.

"Mr Grylls. The interview panel is ready to see you now. Please do come in."

This time the panel is just two – Professor Rogers, rotund, and a Chris Lane, Head of Sculpture, not rotund.

"Well. How do you see your teaching career going?"

"Oh, I intend to be a practising artist, Professor Rogers. First and foremost. Throughout my life."

"Yes, yes. So do we all, what?"

"It is just that I wouldn't want to be a full-time teacher. That is why I applied for this job. But the stimulation of teaching students would . . ."

"Help you as well as the students?" A supportive intervention by Mr Lane.

" Yes. Absolutely. The two go hand in hand. Symbiotic. [Did I really say that?] It is just that I wouldn't want to run a department or even an art school."

"Like I do, you mean?"

"No, no. Someone has to do it, Professor Rogers. And I do think it should always be a practising artist, as you are. That is of course if you want to do it and can do it. My father hired a practising artist to run his art department at the school he was head of. He believed that practitioners should run things like art and music departments in schools. Not just at university level.

"Oh yes? Tell us more."

"Well. It was in Nottinghamshire. He ran a church secondary school. But the school inspectors were not happy with my father as he had appointed a man who was just an artist and hadn't been trained to teach."

I pause. Why are they interested in this? What the fuck has this to do with plastic vacuum forming?

"Go on, please. What happened?"

Well, my father said to the school inspectors that he himself would train the artist to teach, that was easy, but he couldn't train him to be an artist, could he?"

Claude Rogers leans back in his chair. He seems to be enjoying this strange interview. In fact he starts chuckling.

"I say. Your dad obviously shut them up with that. Excellent. What a good fellow."

"Yes. Quite clever. Peter Brannan was the teacher's name. He shows at the Leicester Galleries in London. He is a good painter. Work a bit like Cotman. You know?"

"Yes. I know Cotman. Excellent watercolourist."

" Yes. But not like my work, of course, as you've seen from the slides I sent you."

"No, quite. We've looked at your work. Interesting though, is it not, Chris?"

"Yes, indeed. I think I may have heard of Peter Brannan. Were you taught by him at all?"

"Yes. I was. When I went to my father's school for a year after failing my eleven-plus. His art room was like his studio. Amazing things there – drapery, model theatres. A sort of Aladdin's cave of a studio."

What else can I say?

"My father, though. He retired some years ago."

"Does he paint in retirement?"

"No. He's not an artist. But sometimes he does little cartoon things. Not bad. He reads – not literature. Once my mother asked him why he didn't read literature, and he said because he had read it all. He was an English teacher originally, you see."

Chris Lane leans forward.

"So what does he read?"

"Thrillers mostly. Rex Stout is a favourite. In a pub with a pint on the side. My mother says he is the only man she knows who takes a book for a drink."

"Well, good for him. So . . . What would you like to ask us?"

"Er, the plastic vacuum forming. I've got some photographs here of sculptures I've made using the technology."

Professor Rogers glances through the half dozen 10 × 8in black-and-white photos I have produced. He passes them to Chris Lane.

"Interesting," says Chris. "Plastic books."

"Not to be taken for a drink, what?" interjects the Professor.

They still haven't answered my question.

"So why plastic vacuum forming?"

Professor Rogers glances at Chris Lane and back to me.

"Oh, I do think that's a technical question for sculpture colleagues.

I'm sure it can be answered satisfactorily after this interview somewhere."

They will be in touch. The secretary returns. Can she take me down to the sculpture department where a colleague will be found to explain?

A colleague is found. Now two of us are standing before a huge plastic vacuum former, which has pride of place in its own room. I"ll try again.

"Well, you see. It is quite simple, Vaughan. The fact is we bought it in March because the Fine Art Department had a certain amount of surplus funds at the end of the financial year."

"Oh."

"You are looking rather puzzled, Vaughan. If we hadn't bought it, the University would have cut that money from our budget next year. That would have been terrible."

We stare at the vast machine in silence. I must make another effort. I walk around it slowly. I must appear as fascinated as possible even though I am bored stiff.

"A very impressive machine."

"Yes, isn't it? Sorry. I must shoot off now, Vaughan. But please feel free to wander around before you leave. And . . . good luck with the job."

I wander around the rest of the department. It is all very civilised. Now I am in what is probably the main sculpture studio. Two technicians are at the far side of some large slices of tree trunk spread out on the floor. They are varnishing the tree trunks it seems. Over in a corner is a stack of carved, wooden legs. They look as though they have already been varnished.

"Hello, I'm Vaughan Grylls. I came for interview to teach here. Plastic vacuum forming."

"Oh, yes, We need someone for that. Now we've got that machine. Have you seen it?"

"Yes, thank you. Very impressive. I'll look forward to using it. If I get the job!"

"You won't use it even if you do get the job. We haven't got any plastic to go with it, you see. Too expensive. No budget for that."

"Oh. But . . ."

"Anyway, my friend. What do you think of these? Good, eh?"

He points to the tree trunk slices.

"Yes. Interesting garden furniture sculpture? Who are you making it for? Who is the sculptor?"

"We are, mate. It is garden furniture. We make it in the holidays for a bit of pin money."

I was offered the job but only one day a week of the two days advertised. The other day was given to an artist who stayed there until retiring nearly forty years later. As for me, I was politely sacked the following summer for saying the wrong things to the right people. Describing Reading's Fine Art Department as soporific to the Professor in the Senior Common Room did not help.

NEWPORT COLLEGE OF ART, 1970

Not being able to exist on one day a week teaching, I wrote letters to art schools all and sundry asking for a job. The only one to reply was the Principal of Newport College of Art, Mr John Wright.

"Please sit down. Let me take a look. This is interesting work. Pun Sculptures?"

"Yes. I invented them. At least I think so."

"Well done. Bully for you. So would you explain this one? *Head Case, Book Case* you've called it."

"Oh yes. It is a sort of Freudian Pun Sculpture."

"So do you see yourself lying on Freud's couch?"

"You could say that. Maybe I should be tied to it."

"What – as a piece of Performance Art? It is all the rage now in London it seems."

"It does appear so. But I want to pass over that sort of thing."

"Right. So what are you working on at the moment?"

"Nothing new really. So busy at the ICA, where I'm showing, and now the Young Contemporaries at the Royal Academy. I'm still doing work on the selection committee. I have to get back there today. For a final check. It opens tomorrow."

"Well, I don't want to keep you longer than necessary."

"No, no. It is just that when that is out of the way, I'll have lots of time to make new work and . . . teach here?"

"H'mm . . ."

Down goes his head to hover again over my portfolio. The Principal's hair is exceedingly black. A very pink man with jet black hair. What would a very black man with very blond hair look like? Maybe I could do a piece of work juxtaposing the two. But how would I start? What would it look like? Life-size or maybe bigger? Let's see . . .

The head has looked up. "You seem a bit far away, Vaughan. I was just asking . . . what artwork would you like to do next? In an ideal world?"

"Oh yes. Sorry. Well . . . er . . . actually I would like to invent a restaurant."

"A restaurant? As an artwork as well as somewhere to eat? Could you actually eat there or would it just be something to look at?"

"Oh no. You could definitely eat there, although I'm pretty sure most customers wouldn't be concerned whether it was an artwork or not. Just the quality of the food and the ambience. And lastly the price."

"So you would not care what the general public thought?"

"No. Not really. Just what other artists thought. And maybe art critics, architects. Those sort of people."

"Could that lay you open to a charge of elitism?"

"No, because artists wouldn't care about the quality of the food much. Most artists can't afford to. All they would think about – apart from it being an artwork – would be the price."

"So what would be the title of this gastronomical artwork?"

"*The Social Classes.*"

"Oh. So how would it work?"

"There would be one section for Upper Class Dining and . . ."

"A Buckingham Palace menu? I thought the English upper classes, as well as artists, didn't care much about food."

"Maybe. Posh wines. All in French . . ."

"And the rest?"

"Well, the Middle Class Dining could be, you know, Mateus Rosé and nut cutlets on the menu and maybe Italian sort of stuff as well."

"The sort of stuff you are beginning to find everywhere in London now – if not in Newport?"

"I suppose so."

"And the last dining section? Fish and chips? Pie and mash . . . the menus you will find everywhere in Newport if you join us."

"Well, yes. But this is just an artist's idea. Anyway, I'd make sure the restaurant prices were all pretty much the same wherever you decided to eat. In fact you could have one course in one section and the next in another and . . ."

I am running out of ideas. He has obviously got the point because he has closed my portfolio.

"It's just an artwork idea. I wouldn't actually run the restaurant myself. It would just say outside *The Social Classes by Vaughan Grylls.*"

"Okay, Vaughan. Sounds interesting. I"ll think about your teaching here and thank you so much for coming. Have a pleasant trip back. I'll be in touch if there are two days a week available."

I never heard from John Wright or Newport College of Art again. But at least he had the decency and interest to see me in the first place. Years later I returned to Newport to help validate a new photography degree. Although he had moved on long before, there were still some staff who remembered Mr Wright and his extremely black head of hair.

HOMERTON COLLEGE, CAMBRIDGE, 1971

After being written to by Reading to say that there was no possibility of my one-year teaching contract being renewed, I started looking out for anything going. I came across an advert for a sculpture lecturer at a college in Cambridge I had never heard of. So I filled in an application form and, before sending it off, bunged in a Guardian *review of an exhibition I had just held.*

Homerton College, Cambridge, is a red-brick Victorian pile on the Hills Road. A friend who was at Cambridge University has told me that when he was there it was referred to as the brothel over the bridge. It hardly looks like one to me. Not that I know what a brothel over or under a bridge looks like. Anyway, as far as I'm concerned Homerton College is a women's teacher training establishment that happens to be in Cambridge and I've been called up to teach some of its women how to do sculpture.

"Please present yourself at the Porter's Lodge and ask to be directed to the Art Department," the letter says. So now I am walking down a long corridor and there seems to be a giant striding towards me.

"Hello! You must be Vaughan Grylls. I'm Mike. Mike Bibby. You obviously followed my directions."

I look up. He must be at least 6 feet 7 inches. More if he didn't stoop. Maybe he stoops because everybody he meets is shorter than he is. Or maybe when he was young he didn't want to grow so tall. He has a large moustache, RAF style, and a very posh, booming voice to match.

"Yes. So you are the Head of the Art Department?"

"Yes! Surprised?"

"Er, no . . ."

"No, I don't look and sound like an artist, do I? Let us take a cup of tea and have a bit of a chat in the Combination Room. It's this way."

"The . . .?"

"Probably the Staff Room to you. Senior Common Room in Oxford, of course. But here in Cambridge University, we call it the Combination Room." A sonorous guffaw, head thrown back.

"So Homerton is part of Cambridge University?"

"Yes and no. Usual academic fudge. Don't worry about that one. That is the Principal's job."

A large oak door opens on to a long room full of substantial easy chairs grouped round coffee tables. Through the huge French windows I see a stunning greensward. The soundtrack is the subdued chatter of academics enjoying afternoon tea.

"Let's go over there. Tea? Sandwiches?"

These are very posh cucumber sandwiches. The crusts have been removed.

"Another sandwich? Actually, just help yourself. The, er, thing is, Vaughan . . . Look, I'll come clean. You are the only candidate . . . I don't mean you are the only one who applied . . . no certainly not . . . But as far as I'm concerned you were the only one worth interviewing. That review in the *Guardian*. Excellent!"

"Thank you. But it was just a show at the Greenwich Theatre Gallery. In the corridors. The paper's critic teaches at Reading so . . ."

"No, no. It helps to be well connected. Dame Beryl thought it a hoot."

"Who?"

"Dame Beryl Paston Brown. The Principal. You'll be seeing her in, let me see . . ."

He glances at his wristwatch. ". . . only 15 minutes. Bugger. I wanted you to talk about your work."

"At my main interview? Is that beforehand?"

"Yes. No. Actually, Vaughan, this is the interview."

"Oh."

"Look, old chap. Had a bit of a run-in with the boss not so long ago.

I'm a potter you see, but I had a show of my recent drawings in College. Six foot high each. And six of them. She bloody well didn't like them. But . . . I'm sure she will like you."

"What were they like? Your drawings. For her not to like them?"

"I'll tell you later. Just to say they were searching and serious studies. Just trying to be fearless. No pussy-footing around, what?"

"Did something happen?"

"Did something happen? I should coco! It certainly did! Ghastly. Dame Beryl walks in to the Private View, takes a look at the work and then announces loudly so the whole bloody room can hear, "In the worst possible taste." Then she stalks out! More tea?"

"Yes, thank you."

I turn to gaze out of the window as he pours.

"Beautiful lawn."

"Indeed. Croquet! Do you play croquet. We love a wicked game here. May I take a peep at your portfolio?"

"Yes, of course."

"Or maybe not. Later perhaps. When we have more time. In the department. Although come to think of it I saw enough in that exhibition catalogue you sent to invite you here. Plus that review of course. Any quick questions I can answer before you see the Principal?"

"Well, were I to be offered the post I've applied for, what would you want my priorities to be? Mainly?"

"Oh, sort out the sculpture studio. It is new, you know. We'll take a butcher's later. And join the rest of department colleagues in teaching our foundation course to first years. And teach SCULPTURE! Don't forget that!" Another guffaw.

"I see."

"Good. And, oh yes, there's a bit of preparing the students to teach art in school. Give them some ideas. You know. That is what the students are here for. Officially. And then you can visit them in schools a day a week. See them on teaching practice. Stand at the back of the class and advise them afterwards. That sort of thing. "

"Well, I would not be very good on teaching them how to keep discipline in class."

"Oh, don't worry about that. You have a teaching certificate, don't you. Anyway, that is the Education Department's responsibility. Anyone you see in trouble, let them know."

"My father called it teaching the tricks of the trade. He was a schoolmaster, you see."

"Good. Well. Do you own a car? You'll need one to visit the schools."

"Yes. A Beetle. I came in it today."

"Good. Look. The hour is nigh, I'm afraid. The dragoness's den for you. Dame Beryl. Let me take you there."

Sounds terrifying. Hope she doesn't think I'm in the worst possible taste. Adjust tie nervously. Don't usually wear one.

The Dame is thin with piercing eyes. She walks round her desk, shakes my hand and beckons me to an easy chair. She sits opposite.

"Well, thank you so much for coming to see us, Mr Grylls. We advertised the post once but the person we appointed later declined. So we advertised again. Which is where you come in. Do you have any particular questions?"

"Well, er, it appears that I am the only candidate being interviewed. Is that correct?"

"Apparently so. But that was for the Art Department to decide. Does it concern you?"

"No, Dame Beryl."

"Good. So please tell me about yourself. You were at the Slade?"

"Yes."

"Splendid. A distinguished art school. And now you are teaching at Reading University."

"Yes. But only a day a week."

"So the rest of the time you are making your ... sculpture? I've read a recent review of your work in the *Guardian*. Cannot say I am *au fait* with your sort of sculpture. But a wonderful and supportive review. Well done."

"Thank you, although I didn't write it. It was written by Caroline Tisdall. But I can't afford to spend the rest of the week making sculpture so I'm driving a lorry one or two days a week."

"How interesting. What do you take around?"

"Central heating parts mostly. To people who have recently retired to the seaside. I think they recall their summer holidays in places like Broadstairs, where I seem to go a lot. So they retire there. "

"Go on."

"Well, I know how cold the seaside can be in winter. I spent a year as a child living near Skegness. Chapel St Leonards it was. Terrible in January and February. I lived there with my Auntie Irene. I'm afraid she liked walking – along the beach from Chapel St Leonards to Skegness and back. Eight miles each way. In the winter. Can you imagine? With a twelve-year-old – me – in tow!"

Dame Beryl is laughing. No dragoness.

"Why did you go and live there, Vaughan?"

"Oh, I had failed the eleven plus. It wasn't punishment for that, though."

More laughter from Dame Beryl. This is a second strange "interview".

"Go on, please."

"Father, who was the head of the Church of England secondary modern school in Newark, said it was easier to get a transfer into a grammar school from a secondary modern in Lincolnshire than one in Nottinghamshire where I grew up. Because there were fewer people living in that county I suppose."

"I suppose. So did it work?"

"No. I'm afraid not. I hated being at Skegness Secondary Modern. So I was brought back to attend my father's school where I went for a year – that was great – and then I passed the thirteen plus and was sent to the local grammar school. I wish I had been sent to the tech college. One or two of those who passed were, you see. And they loved it. But I hated the grammar school."

"Why was that?"

"Well, it was trying to be snooty. I've been to seven different types of schools."

"Yes. I noticed that in your application. Interesting. Useful maybe for seeing our students on teaching practice We use all sorts of schools, you see."

Silence. I lean back in my chair. I don't know what else to say.

"Would you care for a cup of tea, Mr Grylls?"

"No, thank you, Dame Beryl. Mr Bibby gave me one in the, er . . ."

"Combination Room?"

"Yes. In there."

"Your father. Did he study here in Cambridge?"

"No. He went to Oxford, actually. But he had to leave after two years as he couldn't afford to stay. That is how he became a teacher. He said that, before the war, it was expensive for a student in Oxford without private money. No grants and living in college was costly and out of college you had to live within one mile of Carfax – the city centre. And so all those places were costly, too. And college friends would think nothing of driving up to London in their sports cars and spending money and everyone was expected to join in. He couldn't afford it. That is what he said."

"Yes. Sadly, I'm afraid it was rather like that. Which college was your father at, albeit briefly?"

"Magdalen. He got a small scholarship from Lincolnshire County Council. There were only two in the county. The other was to Trinity College. You know. In Cambridge."

"Indeed. Well, that is all splendid."

More silence.

"Well . . . Mr Grylls, thank you so much for coming. Should the Art Department decide to offer you the post, you may miss your central heating deliveries to . . . Broadstairs?"

She stands and smiles. So is that it?

"I don't think I would miss driving my lorry to Broadstairs regularly, Dame Beryl. But thank you for seeing me."

She escorts me to the door.

Now I am in a wide corridor and looking desperately for a loo. Just like after that Falmouth interview, although this couldn't have been more different. Was the polite informality just as scary even though there was no dragoness? The loo? I'll ask that student over there.

Flush the loo. The only Men Only in the college. That is what I was told by the student. Open the door . . . and standing at the single urinal is Mike Bibby.

"Hello, Vaughan! Well, the Principal has already rung me and she is very happy so all I need to say now is congratulations – you've got the job. Let me shake your hand. No let me wash my hands first – er, no, you go first. Only one washbasin, what?"

"Thanks."

"My turn, Vaughan!"

"Yes, of course."

"There we are. Well, here we go again . . . Put it there! Congratulations."

"Thank you."

"Right, Vaughan, let me take you down to the Art Department and show you the new Sculpture studio."

I stayed two years at Homerton College, Cambridge, although I could have stayed longer. Mike Bibby was certainly the most supportive person I have ever worked for, but this women's teacher training college was too rarified an environment for me. I wanted to be back in the rough and tumble of London. Indeed, I never moved to Cambridge but commuted from London throughout my time there. As for Mike's "in the worst possible taste" drawings, what did they look like? The Art Department's technical assistant put me right not long after I started. "Oh, cunts, Vaughan! Just great big cunts."

LONDON COLLEGE OF PRINTING, 1973

The London College of Printing, or LCP as it was then known, now the London College of Communications, part of the University of the Arts, is a 1960s office block overlooking London's Elephant and Castle district. The interview I had for a "Principal Lectureship" – doing what exactly I cannot remember – took place near the top floor which offered a splendid view of where Charlie Chaplin was born and raised. I wouldn't have thought it when I first gazed out of the window but my experience here would exhibit all the hallmarks of one of Charlie's films – a pompous character, his come-uppance and a cloyingly sentimental finale.

"Where are you lecturing now?"

I turn from gazing out of the window to see which of the two other candidates shortlisted for the job and sitting opposite waiting for the outcome of our respective interviews has spoken.

"Oh, Cambridge."

"Cambridge? The art school there?"

"No."

"Must be the University. So why have you bothered to come here? Was it the Principal Lectureship grade?"

"No, neither. It's just that I live in London and, well, the college I am teaching at is a teacher training college and, although it is closely affiliated to the university and is very nice, if you like that sort of thing, it is not really for me. I'd much rather teach in London. I'm Vaughan, by the way. Vaughan Grylls. You?"

"Roger Huxtable. "

Roger inclines his head and eyes towards the smaller guy sitting next to him who has been staring glumly at the drab lino on the floor since he emerged from the interview room.

"This is Clive. Clive Pallant."

Clive looks up as slowly as he possibly can. "We know each other," mutters Clive.

"We should do. We are colleagues, aren't we, Clive?" responds Roger breezily, leaning over and placing an unwelcome arm around Clive.

"Yup," says Clive, returning to examine the floor.

"Well," I say, picking up on Roger's breeziness, "they shouldn't be too long making their minds up in there. After all, there are only three of us to choose from."

"There should be only two," mumbles Clive without bothering to look up.

"Now now, Clive," says Roger, "they want to be fair."

Roger and Clive fall silent.

"You said you are colleagues, Roger. Where do you both work?"

Clive looks up quickly and almost aggressively, directed towards Roger and before he can answer, "Here. We both work here. Don't we, Roger?"

Roger nods. "In the same department, Vaughan. Vis Com."

"Visual Communication? The department this job is in?"

"Yeah. And only one of us should have been shortlisted for it. But the Head of Department, Alex – you met him in there – he's a bit of a bastard, isn't he, Clive? Wants to set us against each other. Divide and rule. Bastard!"

"Well, I'm here. They might offer it to me, Roger."

"Vaughan. You are here to make it look right. It is going to be one of us. That's what Alex said."

"Oh, well, if that's the case the only thing stopping me leaving right now is they have my portfolio in there. But I've heard that jobs in London art colleges are usually fixed beforehand. So I'm not very surprised."

"They're not all fixed. Which one of us it will be, for instance. We don't know," adds Clive helpfully.

"No, we don't know," echoes Roger, now looking a little less ebullient.

"I make pun-sculptures. What sort of work do you do?"

"I'm a print-maker," says Roger.

"So am I," says Clive.

"I'm a Senior Lecturer," says Roger.

"I'm just a Lecturer," says Clive. "You?"

"Just a Lecturer, Clive."

The door to the interview room opens. There stands . . .?

"Alex!" exclaims Roger.

"Hullo, Roger," says Alex. But he turns his eyes . . . to me!

"Great interview, Vaughan. But, er, the panel would like to see Mr Pallant." And then, still eyeing me, "Sorry, Roger."

Roger and Clive turn to one another. Stunned is not the word for their expressions. Then Clive gets up, adjusts his tie, draws himself to his full height and strolls through the doorway held open helpfully by Alex the Bastard. It clunks shut.

Silence.

"Bastard. The fucking bastard. I was above Clive. Clive will now be above me!"

"Sorry, Roger. Will he accept? "

"Course he fucking will, Vaughan. It's all right for you."

"Hardly. It appears I was just here as window-dressing."

Roger ignores this. He has more important things to consider. In fact he looks as though he is about to burst into tears.

"They planned this. To humiliate me! I'm a Senior Lecturer! Bastards, the lot of them!"

The door opens.

"I've been offered the Principal Lectureship."

"And?"

"I've accepted, Roger."

Roger bursts into tears, jumps to his feet, clasps Clive and now they are both sobbing. Alex strolls out with my portfolio.

"As I said, Vaughan, a great interview. And great work. Thanks for attending, Vaughan. Here is your expenses form. Just complete it and send it in. I've already countersigned it."

Alex walks over to the sobbers and clasps both of them to him. Now I have a three-man love-in to experience. Pass the sick bucket.

"Great, guys. Terrific, both of you." I get up to leave. Me and the Bastard are the only ones in the room with dry eyes.

In those days, the central London art schools each reported to the Inner London Education Authority (ILEA). Although formal interviews were required by the ILEA, it was common knowledge that in its art schools the internal candidate would be favoured more often than not. So this example was just a little twist on that.

BELFAST COLLEGE OF ART, 1974

Not having been successful in getting a job in London, I now went to the other extreme – a Senior Lectureship in Sculpture at Belfast College of Art. Actually, it was an excuse. I wanted a free flight to Belfast so I could photograph the streets for an exhibition in a London art gallery I was then running with fellow Slade graduate, Nick Wegner. We called the exhibition "Belfast in Art". The plan was for me to shoot a whole roll of 35mm film and then choose the six least interesting images for enlargement and display in our gallery. But we had no money so . . . you never know. There may be a part-time job there, Troubles or no Troubles.

"Where is the college exactly?"

"The main campus is outside Belfast, Mr Grylls. Lovely setting." The Northern Irish tones are strangely reassuring.

"Okay. Well I'll be at the interview and thank you for the flight information. And thank you for inviting me."

"You are very welcome. We all look forward to seeing you."

I hang up. H'mm. Is this a good idea? Going at all I mean.

At Aldergrove Airport I hail a taxi. The flight over was full of the buzz of Northern Irish conversation. Half-asleep, it sounded a lot like American English.

I thrust my papers at the driver.

"Can you take me to the main campus?"

"The art college isn't there."

"Oh? Where is it then?"

"It's in the city sonter."

"The centre?"

"Yes."

"Well, that is where the interviews are. So we'd better go there."

"Okay. We'll be going down the Crumlin Road."

"Right. Is that the quickest way? To the college?"

"Yes. And, if you're interested I can point out where the Red Hand Commandos operated and then Bloody Friday. Terrible things. It's a front line."

Dropped outside Belfast College of Art. Find the interview place. Three interviewers and three interviewees. I don't see any of the other candidates but I am told at my interview that one is an internal candidate and that we are being invited to return at 5 p.m. when they will have made a decision. That is great as it will give me enough time to take thirty-six photos for *Belfast in Art*, see them at 5 and catch the 7 p.m. flight back to London.

And now the interview.

"How long have you been making your . . .?"

"Pun sculptures?"

"Yes."

"About five years, although I'm now running a gallery with a fellow Slade graduate as a continuing artwork – in Lisson Street, London."

"Not the Lisson Gallery?"

"No, but just round the corner."

"Which artists do you show?"

"None. We put on 'Display Exhibitions'."

"Display Exhibitions?"

"Yes. I got the idea from my first visit to New York last year. I went to the Kodak Galleries and I was thrilled by the way they put all their effort into exhibition display and none whatsoever into content. Very Andy Warhol . . . without them realising it."

"What sort of exhibitions do you show?"

"Well, I've devised a display system which can show anything really. The title of the exhibition is important though."

"Such as?"

I pull out our invitation cards.

"*An Indo-Chinese Pun-Sculpture. Drug Abuse in Maine. The Floods in Egypt. Bungalow.* I see. Interesting. What is *Bungalow* like?"

"That one was a pure Duchampian ready-made. I did a day's teaching at Sheffield art school and the polytechnic, of which it is now part – a bit like here – had an exhibition in the foyer of photographs of the history of the bungalow. So I asked the curators of the show whether they would like to show it in London. They were very pleased. So then when they sent it to us we reassembled it to fit our display exhibition format. No artist in sight. The art critics who came to the show were very puzzled. But the sociologists who had put the show together were delighted. They didn't care whether it was art or not."

"Would you say you were very *avant-garde,* Mr Grylls? Pushing the idea of sculpture to its limits?"

"Oh, yes. Very much so."

"You trained as a sculptor, Mr Grylls, but now you seem to use photography quite a bit. How did that come about?"

"Quite quickly. I had to have my sculpture photographed for an exhibition catalogue and when the photos came back, they looked better than the sculptures so I decided to make sculptures that I would throw away when they had been photographed and then I thought . . . why bother? . . . why not just make sculptures out of photographs?"

"Oh, I see. Well, we certainly need some new ideas here. Would you bring them with you?"

"Of course, but I would only be interested in teaching here on a part-time basis. Say two days a week or four days a fortnight? I can then carry on with The Gallery London. That is what we call it."

"Well, we"ll have to think about that."

"Thank you."

"So, you've now got a couple of hours before returning. You can use our library if you like. Or have another look around the art school."

"Thank you, but I'm off to collect some information for another show at our gallery. Called *Belfast in Art.*"

"*Belfast in Art?* How will you do that?"

"Well, I'm going to wander around the city using up a whole reel of film so I'll have just 36 shots I can take."

"There are some places it would not be a good idea to photograph, Mr Grylls. Maybe we should send somebody with you."

"Thank you. But I"ll be okay. I'm looking for the most boring photographs I can find. Then we'll choose the six most boring of the boring for our Display Exhibition."

Out into the street. An army truck with soldiers brandishing guns roars past. There are army checkpoints at all the main road junctions. Finding photographs that are not photo-journalist clichés of the Troubles will be harder than I thought. It is going to be tough to be dull.

Five minutes to five o'clock. A slightly built woman with dark hair and a thin man with a red beard are sitting outside the interview room clutching their portfolios. We nod at one another without speaking.

The interview room door opens. The Head of Department sticks his head round but leaves his body behind.

"Mr Grylls?"

Oh no! Here goes.

"Mr Grylls, we hope you got the photographs you wanted. We do think your ideas are very interesting but would you accept this post provided you taught some, how shall we say, less *avant-garde* sculpture as well?"

"Yes, of course. I can do both – on two days a week or perhaps four a fortnight? Or something like that?"

"I'm afraid we cannot do that. It would mean offering our second-choice candidate a part-time post and that person has indicated already that they are looking for full-time employment. Would you like a few minutes to think about it?"

Relief comes over me. "No. That is the only basis I would accept."

"Too bad. But thank you for coming."

I am escorted to the door and the slightly built woman with dark hair is beckoned.

I still feel cowardly and underhand for not taking that job as advertised and offered. Anyway, they deserved someone better. The good thing is that Belfast was, and still is, a very good art school.

WEST HALL COLLEGE OF EDUCATION, 1974

This Church of England teacher training college in London was in a rather beautiful Giles Gilbert Scott building with a chapel at its centre and impressive lawns spreading down from the Senior Common Room. The feel of the place was similar to Homerton College, but without the Cambridge cachet of course.

"Applications are invited for a one-year Temporary Lectureship in Light and Sound in the Department of Art."

This one looks like another Plastic Vacuum Forming opportunity. From the ad it is obvious they haven't a clue as to what it means at all. So all I need to do is take slides of my pun sculptures and The Gallery London's Display shows, and then project them on to anything really such as, looking round my room in Swiss Cottage, that table, that Victorian chair, that potted palm, that table fan, this desk and this typewriter. Then photograph the result. Easy. As for the sound, I'll find some electronic rubbish somewhere. Or we can sit in silence *à la* John Cage for some of them . . .

"Well, this is just an introductory interview, Vaughan. I'm Sybil Bonham, Head of Department, this is Arthur Cocks who runs Sculpture for us, and this is Ron Grint who, er . . ."

"Runs Painting. I'm a Senior Lecturer."

"So am I," adds Arthur, an older man with darting eyes and a sly, sideways smile.

Ron stares at him briefly. Just a flash of loathing, quickly masked by an exaggerated grin. Arthur impassive. I see. Round One to Arthur . Light and Sound a departmental weapon most likely. Who was it who said fights in academe are so vicious because the stakes are so low?

"I see you are a member of Hampstead Labour Party."

"Oh yes, Sybil. I joined a couple of years ago. What with the election and wanting to . . ."

"Yes, of course."

"And what are you working on now?"

"Well, two things. I have a show coming up at the Ikon Gallery in Birmingham called *Drawing a Lesson From History* – about Watergate, really – and I'm also working with my colleague Nick on the next show at The Gallery London. With light and sound as necessary."

"Oh, yes? That's just a technique, though. Your ideas are more interesting, I feel. Where is your studio?"

"Studio would be a bit grand. Just four garages I rent near our flat in Swiss Cottage. But they serve their purpose. One for making The Gallery London's stuff. One for my own pun sculptures, one for storage, and the last for, er . . ."

"Light and Sound work? Fine. Well. Do either of you wish to ask Vaughan any further questions? No. Okay. You can, of course chat over coffee in the SCR. We can also catch up with the other candidates there. Shall we go?"

Sybil is bright while Rosencrantz and Guildenstern here are just a couple of bozos. But I wouldn't trust either of them.

"So what do you think of this new, wonderful Light and Sound? It's just a technique, as Sybil said. Don't you think?"

Arthur eyes me for a reaction. Careful, Vaughan.

"It is interesting and vital but only if it is based in – extends – sculpture in the traditional sense of a three-dimensional aesthetic . . ."

"What is Arthur asking you? Have you seen our sculpture studio, Vaughan?"

Ron has seen Arthur cornering me and has decided to wander over.

"No, not yet."

Ron slurps his coffee. Arthur impassive again.

"I'm surprised you'll be able to get in the door. The thing is, Vaughan, Arthur doesn't like Light and Sound. Do you, Arthur?"

"Depends what you mean by it, Ron. Do you know what it means?"

Across the room I see Sybil beckoning me. Thank God.

"Vaughan, the Principal and myself will be interviewing you formally at . . ."

She takes out a paper..

"Three o clock. You are number two of the four candidates. Up the main staircase where you came in and at the top turn right. First door on the left. Good luck."

"Vaughan, why don't you and I come down to Sculpture?" says Arthur. "The other candidates have already seen it but you haven't."

Sculpture is in a claustrophobic underground room. Stuff is piled everywhere. It is difficult to move. We could be in King Tut's tomb without the quality artefacts.

"This was all Ron's idea. Usual flim-flam. To get at me. If you come here be careful of him. Terrible lecturer. No, I shouldn't say that. Naughty Arthur!"

That sly sideways look again.

"I'm not just a sculptor, you know. I'm a committed Christian, Vaughan, so I must never cast the first stone. "

Another sly look.

"In fact, I'm in holy orders. But I don't talk about that. We are all sinners, Vaughan. Holy orders or not. Don't you think?"

"I suppose we are – to a greater or lesser extent."

"Well, look. I think Sybil likes you. But Light and Sound. It will take place here – as part of Sculpture. That's the understanding. Sybil backs that. Anyway, I've said too much. Feel free to look around. Toodle-oo."

He is gone. What an unpleasant man. This place looks appalling. When I think what the sculpture studios looked like at Homerton College, Cambridge and at Reading . . .

The sound of steps outside.

"Hi, Vaughan. Arthur hiding in here somewhere?"

"Oh, hello Ron. No. He left about five minutes ago."

"Isn't this appalling? Whoever is appointed will have to bring this into the twentieth century. And it's only a one year appointment. Christ! Actually they won't. They should just ignore it and set up a brand-new Light and Sound studio working with Painting. It will just wither away. No student will want to work here then."

"May I see the Light and Sound studio?"

"Well, no. It'll be part of Painting. The person appointed will decide what they want. Do you want to hear something to make you laugh? Even in here?"

"Okay."

Well, the present principal, Laurence Card – we call him "Larry Who Will Never Marry". You'll see why. He's only been here a couple of years. Before him we had a lady principal. A spinster. She was here from when it was a women's teacher training college. Anyway, I'd just started and I was at this Academic Board meeting and the Principal said that as there were plenty of empty spaces around the college and she wanted to see more sculptures by students displayed could Arthur Cocks arrange it? Of course, Arthur said he could. Nodded like a toy dog he did, Vaughan. Then the Principal said, 'Thank you, Arthur. It is good to know Cocks will now fill anything.' A few in the Academic Board laughed. A few men. There were a few men teaching here then."

Ron has relayed the Principal's comment in a cod upper-class woman's accent. It is obviously a party piece for him.

"Huh. Amusing."

"But, don't you see, Vaughan, don't you see?. . . it was a women's college!"

"Well, it didn't have to be just a women's college to make the joke. Not nowadays anyway."

"Oh, I get it. The present principal. You'll be seeing him soon. Ha ha!"

He squeezes his way towards me between the chairs, tables, plaster moulds, aluminium armature wire and the rest of the clutter to deliver an unwelcome punch to the shoulder.

"You're a wicked one, Vaughan. Great!"

And now the formal interview. An oak-panelled study with Sybil Bonham and the principal. He is in a black leather zip jacket with studs. Lots of talk about my time at Cambridge. In the world of teacher training, Homerton is the bee's knees. Not a dicky bird about Light and Sound, of course.

I am peeing in the "Gentlemen's Toilets (Staff Only)". Relief needed before the successful candidate is summoned. I look around. These gents are more extensive than at Homerton. But then I suppose it is because this is now a mixed college and with more male pricks on the staff. Right. Time to zip up and zip out of here. But then, who comes in but he who will never marry. Larry strides straight to the urinal right next door to me. He stares straight ahead at the tiles.

"Vaughan. I just want to say . . . we would like to offer you the job. But I'll do this formally of course when you join the other candidates and I call you in. Assume you will accept?"

"Er, yes."

"Excellent . . . See you in a few minutes."

The job was as I expected. The terrible duo each tried to use me as a weapon against the other. When I wouldn't play ball, they did their very best to stop my one-year contract being renewed. Unfortunately for me, there was no referee in sight as Sybil left before my arrival and her successor had decided to stick his head in the sand.

But all was not lost. Within a year I had proposed a new postgraduate Art & Design teacher training course in which students from good art schools continued their own work as artists and designers with studio space to match, alongside learning about teaching. I had copied the brilliant course at Goldsmiths. But the price was that Ron was put in charge. Of course, the studio space, central to the vision, did not materialise under him. Three years passed before Ron took a sabbatical and I became the course leader. I then took over the whole department, created studio space, and refused to move when he returned. For several years afterwards, I had the happiest and most fulfilling time I have ever experienced in teaching, with the most wonderful students. That was until the college was subsumed into a new higher education institute and a new head of department arrived . . .

WEST HALL INSTITUTE OF
HIGHER EDUCATION, 1983

By 1983 I had been running the Postgraduate Certificate in Education Art & Design course for five years. I had studio space for each student, a great range of staff, and teaching practice placements in all types of schools and colleges – east London comprehensives, Eton College, Wimbledon School of Art's Foundation course, you name it. So my students got teaching experience across a whole spectrum of British education and also learned something about its variety and, I have to say, unfairness. But in 1982 a new head of the Art Department arrived at West Hall, which by this time had been upgraded to an Institute of Higher Education. His name was Kevin Crumb. I'm afraid it was not long before Ron Grint managed to get himself upgraded to become Kevin's deputy. That meant my lovely course's days were numbered, as were mine!

Standing in my College studio, I turn to the student interviewee and point to a piece of my own work.

"What do you think I should do with this, Frances? The colour?"

"Well . . . you could saturate it more . . . over here. And here . . . possibly these shapes are over-emphasised. Maybe more of a hint. Make it . . . less obvious?"

"Yeah. I see. Why would that be a good idea? Making something less obvious?"

"Er . . . well, then it's more for the viewer to do."

"Why would that be a good idea?"

"Pulls them in more. Makes someone looking at it become more engaged with it. Because they try to work it out. You know. Some parts easy. Others, well . . ."

"I see. And could you explain that to someone who doesn't know much about art, maybe doesn't care – a fourteen-year-old, for example? Maybe a class full of them?"

Frances eyes me. A bit warily. A bit suspiciously. Am I rumbled?

"Well, I think what I would do . . ."

"You are right, Frances. Anyway. Enough about my work. So . . . do you have any questions about the postgraduate course you've applied for?"

"Yes. Well, umm . . . when is the interview?"

"Oh, that. You've just had it. I'm Vaughan Grylls, by the way. The course leader. And I'm offering you a place on our course."

"You are? I thought you were one of the lecturers working in their studio. I was told by the secretary to just come here and wait."

"That is true. My apologies. But my subterfuge is the best way I know to really engage applicants. Anyway. There you are. A place is yours – if you want it, that is. We would like you."

"Well, I want you over here. This afternoon. Half-past three, Vaughan."

Ah yes. Closing time. And a Friday.

"What is it about, Kevin?"

"You'll see. When you get here. A proposition."

I put down the phone on my desk and gaze out the window. My desk faces the window. Maybe because I want to escape? My hands are trembling.

"Shall I come back, Vaughan? Later?"

"No . . . it's okay, Bill. This is okay. I mean this." I gesture at his essay on my desk.

"I'm not good at writing, Vaughan. I'm a Canadian paper-making artist. Maybe an art teacher. In the future. When I've finished your course."

"Well, you have to do the odd essay. For the education department. You know that, Bill."

He nods, stands, walks to the door and turns.

"I know I shouldn't say this, Vaughan, but we don't respect Kevin Crumb. The students on this course don't. We just don't. That stuff of his

– Community Art, he called it. Commissions he's got. For murals in hospitals and things. And the undergraduate students then have to make them for him! Unpaid assistants. That's not art education. We refused when he came down, when you were at the Arnolfini in Bristol installing your show. It was him who rang, wasn't it?"

"Yes. It was indeed. Thanks, Bill."

"We'll tell him again if there is any more trouble for you."

"No, please don't. But I do appreciate the students' concern. I'll be fine."

"Come in! Come in!"

"Afternoon, Kevin."

"Ron's here. Thought you wouldn't mind. An old colleague of yours . . . and . . . to provide another perspective?"

"A propositional perspective?"

Scowl from Ron, smirk from Kevin. Both smell of booze. Ron looks particularly glassy and red in the face, even for him.

"I'll come to the point, Vaughan. How do you see the future of the postgraduate art teachers' course you run?"

"Very good. And popular. Around six applicants for every place. Some good candidates this morning. And they get jobs when they leave. The main thing."

Ron interjects. "It's not what the government wantsh. More teachers. Of art. They have . . . enough."

"What Ron means to say is that Her Majesty's Inspectorate only want to see courses like this at the Institute of Education, Goldsmiths and Hornsey. In London, that is. But not here."

Kevin's beady, black eyes scan me for a response. Ron feigns sorrow while basking in Kevin's protection as his recently ennobled Deputy Head of Department.

"Well, I am very surprised to hear this, Kevin. The course has been running since I introduced the idea in 1975 and it is now 1983. We must challenge it."

"He didn't introduce it. I did."

I ignore the drunken liar.

"Why cannot we challenge it?"

"I'm not challenging it, Vaughan. You are the challenging one."

"Well, I'll challenge it then, if you brief me."

Suddenly Kevin stands up and places himself in front of Ron who remains slouched in his chair.

"What I mean to say, Vaughan, is that you challenge ME! At every turn. I'm not putting up with it any more. I am the Head of the Department of Art. I am a committed and WELL-KNOWN PAINTER, I am a committed COMMUNITY ARTIST and I am sick, sick and tired quite frankly, of your obstructive and SOCRATIC arguments with me. I am sick of you challenging me."

"In what way, Kevin? Can you give an example?"

"You know in what way. Turning off the postgraduates from Community Art."

"But I didn't. They thought for themselves. And they said so. Anyway, Kevin, you've had it in for me since you arrived a couple of years ago. Aided by him. He hides behind you. Literally at the moment. And he didn't invent the postgraduate course. I did and I have the paper trail to prove it."

I cast my eyes away from looking up at Kevin and crane my neck towards his stooge as cooly as I can but my heart is pounding. I feel as though I'm about to throw up.

"You stirred up the postgraduates against me, Vaughan. After that lecture. Which I asked you to give on your own work to the whole department. When you had that one-man show at the Arnolfini Gallery. WHICH I GAVE YOU A WHOLE WEEK OFF TO PREPARE FOR!"

This last part is yelled. The gloves are now off.

"Kevin. The lecture you asked me to give was a set-up because at the end after the questions you stood up and said that photography was not art – that is to say, my art – and it would have no place in your new department which would now concentrate on 'community art' but community art turns out to be commissions you have obtained for murals for hospitals which you have designed and which you then get the undergraduates to make. You've turned this department into a workshop for you! The postgraduates, who are training to be art teachers, just wouldn't have it. So that frustrated you."

Kevin is now also red in the face. I feel I am as well, even though I'm the only one here who hasn't been drinking.

"You stirred the postgraduates up against me. I know. I've done it myself in the past. It is easy. And now you've done it again."

"I have done nothing of the sort. When did I do this, Kevin?"

Ron now feels emboldened enough to join in. Up he staggers to emerge from behind his master, thick with drink.

"Vaughan. When Kevin outlined his . . . er . . . plans for the department after . . . er . . . generthlly . . . thorry generously giving you the time off for an exhibition installation and then a lecture on it here, I have reason to believe you got some of the students, maybe not all of them . . . pothgraduates – I don't know, but that is beside the point – you got them to . . . stick photocopies of your reviews from the exhibition all over his office door. Keith was too polite to say anything about such . . . well . . . sheer . . . er . . . eff, eff . . . effrontery."

"I did not, Ron. Even though they were good reviews. Did you read any? The *Sunday Times*, the *Observer*, the . . ."

"Vaughan. You are trying to show up Kevin . . . who is a well-known . . . a well-known . . ."

"Cunt?"

Kevin spins round at Ron and then back at me. He is livid. Will he hit me? If he does, I am ready and he is drunk.

"Ron, just sit down. This interview is now over, Vaughan. FOR THE TIME BEING, VAUGHAN! OVER! Get out!"

"Interview?"

"Get OUT!"

As I close the door, he shouts superfluously, "I'LL GET YOU, YOU FUCKING BASTARD!"

As I drove away, I had to pull over. My hands were shaking too much to steer. And I could hardly see where I was going as I was weeping. All I could think about was the new students coming next year and that I could not let them down even though the course I worked so hard on was doomed. Next year would undoubtedly be its last and I and my staff would be made redundant. I had to start looking for a new job, something I hadn't done for nearly a decade. But where and how should I start?

MASSACHUSETTS COLLEGE, 1984

In 1984, thanks to Mrs Thatcher's new medicine for the UK economy, there were few jobs going in the UK's art schools. That was not surprising as it was now policy to contract the public sector, including higher education, a situation used at my expense by Kevin Crumb. I did get visiting teaching in some art schools, such as Farnham, thanks to my 1983 exhibition at the Arnolfini and its positive reviews but, however rewarding those jobs were, they did not meet the costs of a family and a mortgage. So off I went on spec to my first College Art Association of America Annual Conference in New York. There I found jobs aplenty. I applied for three and was offered an interview at two, one in California, the other in New England. As I couldn't afford to travel to both, my initial reaction was to go to the California interview even though it was only a one-year contract whereas the New England one was three. But friends in New York persuaded me otherwise, saying that the New England job was not only near New York City (by which they meant a three-hour drive, short by North American standards) but that the university was a top liberal arts college. I did not know what American liberal arts colleges were as there is no direct equivalent in the UK, then as now. The nearest would be to say that they are a cross between an exclusive public school and an Oxbridge college. The students, who were mostly undergraduates, went on to graduate courses at America's top Ivy League universities – Columbia, Harvard, Princeton and Yale – or took a job at a smart Wall Street firm, sometimes owned by daddy. These liberal arts colleges were very prestigious, very rich and their students very bright and usually very white.

DAY 1. THE PROVOST'S OFFICE.

The Provost, Professor Chester Defaux, flicks through what he calls my resumé.

"So you've been teaching graduate school?"

"Yes – graduate Art & Design students training to teach. And I also teach at Farnham. The Photography degree course. And I do visiting talks about my shows."

"I see."

"You see, some art schools only want to hire someone who has only been teaching the subject of photography in other art schools. I do that as well, of course."

"Well, you don't need to be defensive about that at all, Vaughan. We take teaching very seriously here. So if you have been teaching teachers to teach, that sounds good to us. I hear you gave a good talk about your work to the Art Faculty. And Bernard Bohm attended. He's our Chair of English Literature here. Not that I know much about English Literature. I'm a simple math guy."

"Yes. My brother David let him know I was coming over here for interview. David met him at an English and American literature conference in England. When Professor Bohm was on a sabbatical at Oxford, I believe."

"Sure. Bernard was indeed in Oxford. Did you know we are developing a campus in England?"

"No."

"Nobody in the Art Faculty mention it?"

"No."

Chester Defaux opens my press clippings book.

"I like these reviews. *The Sunday Times*. The *Guardian*. The *Observer*. I take the *Manchester Guardian* weekly. We still call it that here. Manchester. That's in the north. Can't say I've been to Manchester."

"Yes. I guess it's a bit like Philadelphia. Or maybe Baltimore?"

"I hope not Baltimore."

More thumbing through my collection of what constitutes my life now laid out on his desk.

"I see you are an alumnus of the Slade School of Fine Art, University

College London?"

"Yes. Some time ago now . . . around fourteen years ago!"

"Okay. Sure. Tell me about yourself. Why do you want to come to America? Why here?"

"Well, as you can see a lot of my work is about America. Maybe in the nineteenth century I would have wanted to go and live in England as that was the centre of the world. But in the twentieth it's America. And I think it will be for some time."

"And here?"

"Well, the specification for setting up a new photography and video department sounded really exciting because I try to push at the boundaries of photography and video, maybe because I never learnt them formally. I trained as a sculptor and I just had to figure out new ways of doing things myself, and that shows in my work and what people write about it, I suppose. It's my strong point."

I try and gauge his reaction. Why did I mention "my strong point"? He's now going to ask, "If that's your strong point what are your weak points?" That's usually the drift in interviews. Better get in first.

"As for my weak points, well I suppose I . . ."

"Hey, I don't want to know about those, Vaughan. We all have those. What I want to know about are your strong points and how you are going to make them even stronger. We would like to help you make them strong for the benefit of Massachusetts and the benefit of yourself should we decide to hire you."

Okay Vaughan. You are in America. Toot your own horn.

"Well, as I said, I am innovative, I am hard-working. I am focused. I am driven. I'm a perfectionist. And my students say I am an exciting and inspiring teacher. And I know the students here have very high scores academically and I think I can excite and stretch them, not just in photography and video, but also in other art forms in the Art Department, should the opportunity arise."

He nods, sort of noncommittally, and pushes his chair back from the desk. Christ. I've overdone it. I glance around the plush surroundings, the leather chairs, the huge, oak, leather-topped desk. The grandfather clock in the corner. The view of the college chapel out of the window. I am now gazing out of the window somewhere else.

"That chapel. It was modelled on a church in Lincoln, England. Do you recognise it?"

"No, I can't say I do. But it's very elegant. I know Lincoln Cathedral. And its wonderful west front."

"How's that? What does that look like?"

"Do you have a pencil and a piece of paper?"

"Sure."

He pushes them across the table. I sketch out the west front, as far as I can remember it, of Lincoln Cathedral. An apt case of, God, I hope it goes like this.

"They put this up, to help support the towers at the front or just for show or most likely a bit of both. It's a one-off design. But it's worked for . . . maybe eight hundred years? Lincoln Cathedral was the tallest building in the world for centuries."

"Really? Next time I'm in England I"ll make sure I get over there. May I keep this?"

"Of course."

Anyway, he's already taken it to check how wrong my memory is. It doesn't matter. I will have been hired or not well before that.

"Vaughan, do you have any questions about the position here?"

"Well, there wasn't any indication of remuneration on the advertisement as I remember."

"What do you make at the moment?"

"About £9,000 a year. And I sell work. Over the last year, about £6,000 worth."

"It won't be less than $28,000, maybe more. Put it this way, if we decide we want you, money will not be an issue."

I meet his eye and in embarrassment return my gaze to that ersatz church. Pounding heart and the pound at par with the dollar.

All these eighteenth- and nineteenth-century buildings. No patina of age on any of them and all plonked down on perfectly manicured lawns.

"So, Vaughan. Who else do you need to meet?"

I glance down at the list and times I've been given by Ann-Marie, the Art Department secretary, with her handwritten note still stuck to the top left-hand corner: "Hi Vaughan, Here's your go-to list – Names, Who Is,

Places, Times. With map and parking. Any probs call 458 2334. Good luck! Best, Ann-Marie."

"Well, Roger Smith the, er, director of the Jackson Institute at 4 p.m."

"Oh, yes. He is one of your countrymen, you know."

"So I hear. This morning Professor Fiona Rein and Professor Anna Shoefish for breakfast at the White Rabbit Retreat. Tomorrow, Professor Tim Whitebrook the printmaker for breakfast at Howard Johnson's, then lunch with Professor Al Altman, the chair of Studio Art at the Faculty Club and then dinner with Kip Kranzler, the director of the College Museum of Art, at his house."

"Okay, Vaughan. So quite a list. Good luck with all of those."

He escorts me across the grand office to the door.

"Thank you for stopping by. I truly appreciate it, Vaughan."

I step out into the picture of perfection that is Massachusetts College. Appreciate it? Are these interviews or just chats? I know the answer. The posher the place, the more seemingly informal the interview. St Paul's, the Slade, Reading, Cambridge. Even Undergraduate Tours. Now here. Like being admitted to some posh club. They wouldn't even take a look at you unless you had been heavily sifted beforehand. They already know you can do the job. The process of the interview is just to see whether they can get on with you. Whether your face fits. Whether you are 'the right type'."

The Jackson Art Institute.

"The director will be right with you. He's just taking a call . . . oh, here he is coming now . . ."

"Vaughan? Hello, I'm Roger. They thought we should meet as fellow Brits! I liked your lecture. Very interesting."

"Pleased to meet you, Roger, and thank you for seeing me. Ann-Marie suggested we meet. I'm glad she did."

"A good thought."

" I didn't know you came to my talk."

"No, you wouldn't have. I slipped in at the back just after you had started with your slides . . . and then I had to leave before you took questions. Sorry about that, but I had to play hookey just to get there! Not easy to slip away given my height!"

Roger is a tall, rangy man in a tweed jacket and tie. He looks and sounds like an Englishman – something I wouldn't have noted, other than here.

"This museum, Roger. I've just spent an hour looking round. I'm glad I did. It is amazing. Rubens, Turner, Picasso, Degas, Cézanne. You name it. And all excellent examples. How did it come to be here?"

"The founder and his wife. Very rich and very discerning collectors. With the assistance of the very best New York dealer of his day."

"I see. But why here? It is beautiful but not exactly central."

"True, but that was the point. They were paranoid about losing their collection to a nuclear attack in the 1950s. That is also why this place is built like a nuclear bunker."

"Seriously?"

"No, I'm being serious."

"Where are they now?"

"Over there. In front of the Institute. Under those two unmarked marble blocks."

"Safe from nuclear attack?"

"Exactly. Coffee?"

"Thank you."

"Are you sure you don't want a sandwich or something?"

"No, thank you Roger, I'm fine."

"So . . . what would you like to know about the Art Faculty? By the way, you may know this already, but when they refer to faculty in America, they mean the academic staff. "

"Well, most of them seem to be art historians."

"Indeed. And some very good ones. The top ones have now retired, of course. They created the American Art Museum Mafia."

He smiles and leans back, sipping his coffee. I am being expected to react.

"Mafia, Roger?"

"The people who now run America's top art museums are more often than not alumni of this university. Just look at the Brooklyn Museum, New York's Museum of Modern Art and the National Gallery of Art. Then there's, let's see . . . Los Angeles, Pittsburgh, Cincinnati, Chicago . . . that's enough to be going on with. Would you like a detailed tour of the Institute tomorrow?"

"I would love to but I just don't have the time, unfortunately. They've really packed out my schedule over these two days. "

"Well, that means they are taking you seriously. They don't do things by halves here."

"I'm sure, but there doesn't appear to be any other candidate."

"Oh, there are perhaps three, but you won't see them. They interview candidates separately in American universities. What else would you like to pick my brains about?"

"Thanks. Yes . . . what about what they call Studio Art – painting, sculpture, printmaking, photography, and architecture apparently? How does the practice of art making and teaching fit in, given all this attention to art history?"

"The poor relation, I suppose. But poor only in relation to a very rich one. The real pecking order is the Art Department as a whole in relation to the redeveloped College Museum of Art. You will have seen that?"

"Yes, briefly. Impressive."

"It is. Kip Kranzler developed it. He used to teach printmaking in the Art Department, didn't get tenure, so moved to what was then a two-bit college museum and what he has done in the last five years is truly amazing – getting funding from all sorts of sources. He is a real mover and shaker and his new museum sits in more ways than one on top of the Art Department. They are almost like his tenants."

"A sort of poetic justice?"

"Some may say so."

"I'm scheduled to see him later."

"Good. I'm sure you'll get on. Is there anything else you would like to know? Anything at all?"

"Well, they reckon the successful candidate will have a new studio built for them and to their spec."

"Ah ha."

"Oh yes, and that although this is just a three-year initial contract, it could be extended into tenure track and then the fourth year would be a paid sabbatical – either a whole year on half-pay or six months on full pay. In other words, a sabbatical is every four instead of seven years. In England now you are lucky to get anything . . . other than a permanent one following redundancy!"

Roger laughs.

"I have no doubt, Vaughan, that what they say about the studio and the sabbatical they mean. This college is a well connected and wealthy institution – as are some of the people in it. No – forget that. I should not have said that."

"Why not?"

"A bit unfair. Look, just read *Who's Afraid of Virginia Woolf* . . . that's if you haven't already.

"Oh yes . . . I remember the film. Burton and Taylor as a couple trapped in an endless fight in a posh New England liberal arts college where he is a professor?"

"Indeed, Vaughan. Indeed."

DAY 2. HOWARD JOHNSON'S.

Professor Jim Whitebrook is small, red-haired and teaches printmaking. Or did, it turns out.

"Hi, Vaughan. I'm Jim. Sorry about meeting here at HoJo's. I'm afraid it's a case of ships crossing in the night. I just wanted to see you before I left."

"Oh? Why are you leaving, Jim?"

"I wasn't going to get tenure. Al Altman made that clear. But I am one of the other main studio art guys. I and our sculpture guy, Denis Slate, who isn't here today – Denis sends his apologies and his wishes for your good luck by the way – eventually persuaded Al to stop dragging his feet, get you over for interview and hire you. The place needs someone like you. He thought your work and your students' work was knock-out."

A waitress hoves into view. "Coffee?"

We both nod. Jim looks at the menu. "I'll take two eggs over easy with a side order of bacon. Nothing else."

"Make that two, please."

"You've got it."

"I love the way the English say 'please' after everything and 'thank you'. It's so sophisticated. I was in London once. Loved it. Can't understand why anyone would want to live anywhere else. Vaughan, you're looking a little worried."

"No, it's just that, it's just that . . . what are you going to do, Jim? After running printmaking for how long, three years?"

"Five. Actually I was here just before Altman. He got tenure in three. But, then, that guy's a schmooze-machine. Me, I'm going back to D.C. I may start a picture-framing business."

"After being a professor here for five years?"

"Yeah. That's America, Vaughan. We're a new country. Things can change fast."

"I suppose so. That's one of the things I like about America, though. You can reinvent yourself. The future is more interesting than the past."

"Maybe. Look. I hope it really works out for you and your family here, Vaughan. Actually I know you'll be just fine."

"But I'm still being interviewed. They may not want me."

"They'll want you, all right. They just have to hire you. They would be crazy not to. I'll put in my word for what it is worth. But if you do show up to work here, just keep your eyes open and think Altman. And his wife, while I'm at it. She's a conceptual artist. Just a tip."

"Here we go, guys! Two over easies. Two side orders of bacon. More coffee?"

Faculty Club dining room.

"Great talk, Vaughan. Students seem to like it. Important. They pay the bills! Anyway, how's it going so far? I guess you've been a busy bee! All these meetings," Al chuckles. He has piercing blue eyes and a Zapata moustache.

"It's fine, Al, just fine. I've seen the Provost. And this morning at ten-thirty the photography major who's acting as an assistant this summer, Ian Lenz, showed me round the photo studio and the repairs needed to get it up and running."

"Yeah, it has been neglected. Have you any idea of cost to fix it up, provide new equipment? I guess not coming from England."

"Perhaps a three-thousand dollar budget to fix it this summer – maybe less. Enough to teach basic photography courses in the first semester, should I be hired. Then establish a budget and order up the equipment for the photography stuff for colour work and of course the stuff for the video studio, both to run from the spring semester."

Al nods. "Sounds like a plan. Ann-Marie has quite a list of people who want to see you, I hear."

"Oh yes, I saw Roger Smith at the Jackson yesterday. And today I had breakfast with Jim."

I slip that one in to see his reaction. For a split second the piercing blue eyes lock on.

"Oh, great. You will have had a perspective from Jim. So . . . who else have you still to see, Vaughan?"

"Kip Kranzler. He's invited me to his house for dinner tonight. Apparently he let Ann-Marie know yesterday."

"Oh, really? Kip's the director of our College Art Museum. He's got his finger in so many pies. Wow! I've never been invited to dinner at his house. Where did that come from?"

"I suppose he wanted to see what a strange beast the department was considering bringing over."

"Yeah. Right!"

Collective chuckling. Al leans across the table to take my hand.

"Hey, I've gotta run. Just to say, good luck, Vaughan. Loved your work. As for your students' work. Pow Vaughan! POW!"

Soft punch to the arm and he is gone.

Kip Kranzler's house.

"It used to be a frat club. Nobody wanted it. That's when frats were closed down here. I rented it. Later I bought it. Another margarita?"

Kip moves to the counter to mix three more before his girlfriend Sally, preparing dinner, says, "Hey Kip. Hold that margarita for me. I don't need another. I won't be able to fix dinner. You mix them so strong."

Kip shrugs. He is huge. Like the house. Everything on a massive scale.

"We're having a faculty show in the Museum of Art. In the fall. If they hire you, I hope you can bring two of your big pieces over. *Greenwich Mean Time* perhaps and the other one, what was it, the British Museum Egyptian section piece?"

"Oh yes, *Britain Through the Looking Glass* it's called. It was very interesting making that work. I had to get special permission to photograph the Egyptian Mummy Room very early in the morning, long before the public arrived."

"Sounds fun. How big is that?"

"They are both twenty-eight feet by eight feet. *Greenwich Mean Time* is a sort of wheel of fortune, a mandala, a wrist-watch, all about time and my place in it, and *Through the Looking Glass*, well, that's also auto-biographical in a way about Britain, you know. Britain collected evidence of one of the earliest empires, Egypt, at a time when it still was an empire itself and, as time passes and my daughter's in it as Alice, that's why it's called *Britain Through the...*"

Kip interrupts. "Sure. I like to hear all that, but those works would look just great in the museum. I'd hang from the ceiling the *Greenwich* piece, and the other one on the wall. In the main gallery. It would take them."

"From the ceiling?"

"Yeah. We've got the technology to do that. A piece of cake."

I look at him as he downs his second margarita. How does he know about these works?

"Oh, Jim told me about your resumé and portfolio. You've met him, haven't you. And have you met Reynard Kempinski, my deputy director?"

"No. I'd like to but I'm returning to New York tomorrow. Then London."

"No problem. I asked him to research your stuff for me. I then told Al they should think of hiring you. You want to be a player here?"

I nod.

"Yeah, you should. That studio Art Department needs some move-ment behind it. I couldn't get it moving. That's why I went into the museum. And now the Museum of Art has a several million dollar endow-ment. You'll take another margarita or wait for the zinfandel with dinner?"

"I'll wait for the zinfandel."

"Sure. By the way, do you know Anthony D'Offay?"

"I know of him. He has a smart gallery in London's West End and shows a lot of interesting artists. Gilbert and George and so on."

"Yeah, well, that's why I raised it. We're acquiring a big Gilbert and George for the museum and I got some installation plans I need to share with you after dinner and, if possible, I'd like you to take them over to

Anthony when you return to London. Would that be okay?"

"Of course."

Sally plonks down dinner. A huge bowl of interesting-looking spaghetti with a salad. The zinfandel appears.

I returned to England and time passed. I assumed I had not got the job. But one day, while I was at home, the phone rang. It was the Art Department chair. He offered me the job on an excellent salary. Could I start in August? Of course I could! He apologised for the length of time in getting back to me and then said that studio art colleagues had been making lengthy considerations. I found out some months later, from another studio art colleague, that it was Al Altman who had been dragging his feet and that they had collectively insisted I was appointed. He had agreed – reluctantly.

WEST HALL INSTITUTE OF
HIGHER EDUCATION, 1984

Having been offered the job in America, I now had to go back for another interview with Kevin Crumb, not least to get a redundancy payoff at some stage, for I knew he and Ron Grint had been planning just that. I had been tipped off by a lecturers' union representative who had seen a confidential document.

"Come in, Vaughan. Take a seat. What can I do for you?"

"I've been offered a job in America, Kevin."

Kevin's little blackcurrant eyes, normally dead, suddenly gain life.

"Oh. Well done, Vaughan. Whereabouts?"

I tell him. "Heard of it?"

"Oh yes, I have, Vaughan. It's a very posh liberal arts university. They haven't written to me for a reference though."

"I didn't give you as a reference, Kevin. I gave Farnham. And also the Principal."

"Well, you got the job. When do you start?"

"Well, that depends on you, Kevin."

"Vaughan, as far as I'm concerned you could start there rightaway. You know that."

"I do, Kevin, I do."

"Well?"

"Well . . . I want to try it out first. It's a three-year contract."

"And? What are you trying to fucking say, Vaughan?"

"Okay. This is what I am trying to fucking say, Kevin. I'll accept the position if you hold my job open here for at least twelve months. That's in case I want to come back if I don't like it over there."

"I can't do that. You either take that job or you don't. And if you don't, there may not be a job for you here in a year's time."

"The thing is, Kevin, if you don't guarantee my job here in a year's time I won't take the job in America. That means I'll be around you here for at least another year or so. So I am just taking unpaid leave of absence. All you have to do is agree that."

The blackcurrants are now swivelling. I have got him.

"Okay, if that's the way you want to play it. What do I have to do?"

I take out a typed letter and shove it across the table. He hardly bothers to read it.

"There. Signed. Enjoy America."

"Thank you, Kevin. I'll try."

Obliging Kevin to keep my job open meant I received a redundancy pay-off the following year when nearly everyone in the Art Department was made redundant, other than Kevin and Ron of course, plus a couple of compliant others. I had escaped, if only just.

MASSACHUSETTS COLLEGE, 1988

Although my job was initially a three-year contract with a fourth year as sabbatical, I had to decide what to do for the future. Tenure applications in American universities are considered after seven years or so, usually when you have completed two contracts, but there was a clause allowing "early decisions" on tenure. As I had very good evaluation scores from my students and a good research track record with my exhibitions of new work, I thought, well, why not? But I had not factored in the collapse of my marriage and the fact that my ten-year-old daughter was back in England and I was flying frequently across the Atlantic to see her. So I had not thought things through. That may have told against me.

"Hi Vaughan. Take a seat. Thanks."

"Hi Al. What is this about?"

"What is it about? As the new department chair I have to interview you about your tenure application."

"Okay."

"Well, we can offer you another year. You've having one already on top of the three-year contract we gave you originally – your sabbatical this year. So that makes five years. By the way, why haven't you been away from the college much during your sabbatical? I went to Spain when it was mine. For the whole year!"

"I know, Al. You asked me to run Studio Art for you in your absence, which I did."

"You did, Vaughan. For which I thank you again."

"Well, Al, as for not going away much this year, I've been undertaking that big commission for the college's sports arena. You know that."

"Okay. But who commissioned it?"

"A college trustee, Mr Sidney Petersen, commissioned it."

"Oh, right. And you are being paid for that over and above your college remuneration?"

"Yes. Anyway, I've applied for tenure. I thought you said that is what this interview is about."

"Well, that *is* what this interview is about, Vaughan and . . . I have to tell you now, Vaughan, and it is not easy for me . . . that your tenure application has been denied. I'm sorry."

I am speechless. I don't believe I am hearing this. Like hell he is sorry.

He leans back, staring me out as best he can. Those piercing blue eyes.

"But . . . I don't understand."

"What don't you understand, Vaughan?"

"Tenure decisions are based on teaching scores and, in the case of the visual arts, exhibitions etc."

"Correct."

"But my student feedback scores – my teaching scores – are the highest in Studio Art. I know that because they are circulated by the college."

"Well, maybe."

"Not maybe. They are, Al."

"That is as it may be. That is what I meant. The fact is, Vaughan, the tenure committee did not feel you had made and exhibited enough high-quality work since you joined us in 1984."

"What? Al, I don't believe this. I had a retrospective show at that great mid-western university you are an alumnus of in 1985. And then there was the catalogue and that essay by John Laurence from Rutgers University. And it got all those reviews – admittedly in the mid-west. But what about that national review of my show in *Art in America*? It was extensive."

"The committee felt that most of the work in that exhibition you had made before you came to America."

"Yes, of course. That *was* a retrospective, for Christ's sake."

He shrugs.

"Al, you said to me, when I had been offered that show within twelve months of arriving here, that it was all right for some and that you had never been offered a retrospective by them even though it was your old school."

"Did I say that, Vaughan?"

"You did, Al. You certainly did."

"So . . . are you implying personal jealousy has impeded your tenure application? "

I am seething with anger at the injustice of this bizarre interview. Carry on, Vaughan. Shame him.

"What about the mural I made for that Channel 4 documentary about my work? *Manifest Destiny*, if you remember. That work was huge in scale, I made it here and it was shown in Plymouth, England, and near Plymouth, Massachusetts – Duxbury, to be exact. And the documentary was not just shown in England but on PBS here. In fact it has been aired every Thanksgiving since 1986."

"The committee felt that your TV show was arranged before you arrived here and many of the images in the mural you made were based on photographs you had taken in Plymouth, England before you arrived here."

"Of course, Al. But three-quarters, the American photos, were taken here since I arrived here and the whole work was made here in my studio."

"The committee also felt you hadn't utilised your college studio enough."

"What, Al? Who advised them of that?"

"I did. I have the studio next door, remember?"

"So you were spying on me. That is appalling, Al, apart from it being wrong to say I didn't use my studio enough. Anyway, even if I didn't, what has that to do with making and exhibiting work? It is irrelevant."

"I'm sorry, Vaughan, but that was not the view of the tenure committee."

"Al, what about my one-man show last year in Chicago where . . ."

"One-*person* or solo . . ."

"Whatever, and then the commissioned college mural? Al, I have made, exhibited and had reviewed more work in three years than the rest of the Studio Art faculty put together. That is a fact!"

"Vaughan. That is also arrogant and quite frankly . . ."

"This is absurd . . . and the external assessors wrote excellent references. Al, I know. They sent me copies."

"Did they? Well. Those are supposed to be confidential. The tenure committee also had its own external assessors."

"What? There was no mention of that in the application form. But if so, just who recommended those people?"

"I did."

"You did? I see. So who are they?"

"I'm not at liberty to divulge that, Vaughan. Privy information."

"Al. This so-called interview with you is simply Kafkaesque."

"I hear you. But you have been made an offer of continued employment for one more academic year. So, rather than prolonging this interview, get back to me with your decision by noon Friday. Okay? Tenure denied. Interview over."

Should I lean over the desk and punch him? Or just walk out as a coward would? A coward walks out.

What the hell was I thinking of, applying for a permanent position given my personal situation? Not getting much sleep that night, next day I went straight to see the Dean of Faculty, Dr Leonard Gerter. I explained, blow by blow, what had happened between me and Al Altman. I then handed in my resignation, to take immediate effect. Leonard was truly shocked and offered me any reference I would care for. That was very kind of him, but for me, America was now over.

KENNINGTON COLLEGE OF
ART & CRAFTS, 1988

The job was Head of College, called that since the art school became part of a large London higher education institution while I was in America. I was surprised I was invited for interview at all. The college's historical reputation was in the crafts rather than fine art and certainly not in photography. But they paid for my return flight across the Atlantic and I had some vaguely sentimental feelings for the place. It was right opposite where I had my studio before I left for America. But things had changed for art schools in the four years I had been away, as I was about to find out. The Thatcher government required the public sector, or what was left of it, to become thrusting businesses, or at least make an effort to ape how they imagined thrusting businesses to be . . .

In an immaculate suit, he holds open the door as we three candidates file into a waiting room next to what is still called, according to the sign on the door, the Principal's office.

"Of course, this is a key appointment. To the Vice-Chancellor. Please wait here. We'll be seeing you, Evelyn, first. Then you, Peter, and . . ."

He consults the paper in his other hand.

"Vaughan. Yes?"

I nod.

"Great. Any questions I can answer before we get going on this?"

"How many are on the interview panel?" says Evelyn.

"Just four. No worries."

"And who are they?" says Peter.

"Oh, the VC . Vice-Chancellor, of course. He's Douglas Malcolm, plus a governor, an external assessor and myself."

"And what do you do?" says me.

"Oh, me? I'm the smallest beast in the circus – just Director of HR, Human Resources."

"What is that? I've been in the States too long!"

The smallest beast looks at me like a rabbit caught in the headlights.

"Personnel. Staffing it was called before that. But you've been in the States. HR comes from there! Ha ha!"

"Maybe, but it is not used in their universities. As far as I know."

"Right. Okay. Let's get started. See you in a few minutes, Evelyn. I'll pop out and call you when they're ready."

"So, Vaughan. You ran a department here and then in the US? And before that a small company? And a gallery?"

"Yes, the department here was the PGCE Postgraduate Certificate in Higher Education in Art & Design. I set that course up. In America, it was the Studio Art Department which I ran for a year when the tenured professor was on sabbatical. That is the academic bit, anyway."

The Vice-Chancellor leans back. He nods towards the man he has introduced previously as Mr Graham, the external assessor. The VC now adds triumphantly:

"Bob Graham is very senior in Marks & Spencer. Bob, your question of the candidate?"

"Okay, Vaughan. Can I call you that?"

"Sure, Bob."

"I love 'sure'! Sounds like the States, Vaughan. Okay. What I want to drill down to is you say here in your CV that you helped run a family company which landed at your door in the 1970s. Tell me more. Sounds interesting."

"Well, it wasn't that interesting. Not like academia – being responsible for the growth of a student. It was just a family business."

"Okay, Vaughan. I'll ignore that. Business being less demanding than the academic world."

"I didn't say less demanding. Bob. May I call you that?"

"Okay, okay. Point taken. Carry on please."

"Well, it was just a small outfit. Made lab apparatus and supplied chemicals, mostly to schools, in the Midlands. It was set up by a great uncle, and my mother called me in when his wife died. The great uncle had died long before. So it had been drifting for years. It was in a poor way. The bank was about to foreclose."

"And you did what?"

"I went to see the bank manager!"

The VC slaps his hand on the table and roars with laughter. He turns to Bob.

"Carry on, Bob."

"Will do, Douglas . . . So. What did the manager say?"

"He said if you don't write a business plan I can approve, I'm fore-closing the loan, so I said what is a business plan, and he said easy. Get three sheets of paper. On the first write down what the firm is doing now. On the second write down what it should be doing to stop losing and make money, and on the third write down how you are going to get from the first piece of paper to the second."

"That was it?"

"Yes, that was it. And he helped me do it. He had to. I'd never heard of a business plan before. I was an artist and an art lecturer. Pretty dumb in such matters."

More roaring and table-slapping from the VC. I seem to be getting somewhere.

"Well," asks the VC, "Did it work?"

"Yes. For a few years. I would spend a day a week up in Nottingham. Eventually my mother sold the company to its largest supplier. Not for much, but at least we kept it going through a tough time for small busi-nesses – the late seventies, early eighties."

"Before Margaret got a good grip on the country," adds Bob.

I don't reply to this as I feel Mrs Thatcher did a huge amount of dam-age to small businesses. Silence.

"Okay, Vaughan. One final question from me," says Bob.

"Yes?"

"How many people have you sacked?"

"Excuse me?"

"Have you ever sacked anybody?"

"Well, I can't say it is the sort of thing I've ever added up. It is not something I would necessarily be proud of."

"Why not?"

"I think it shows failure in a way. Especially if you've hired the person yourself. Whether they are students, or visiting lecturers or . . ."

"Never mind about students. What about staff? Managers in particular. Did you sack the manager at the company your family inherited?"

"Unfortunately, yes. Then the sales manager. And some others in my academic life . . . part-time lecturers, etc."

"Thank you. And you could do it again?"

"If I had to, Bob. Depends why and where."

The VC interjects. "Here. Bloody here!" He leans forward.

"Let's get to the point, Vaughan. My heads of college need to identify pretty quickly those who don't contribute to the success of their college and therefore the institute as a whole and . . . sack 'em. If they don't, I will not hesitate to sack that head of college who I think is dragging their feet. I do not want to be surrounded by non-contributers. How do you feel about that?"

I look across the desk at the four men, two of whom, sitting either side of Malcolm, have said nothing throughout the whole interview.

"I understand you would only want people right next to you, Vice-Chancellor, who are clearly contributing."

Marks & Spencer man turns his head downward and smiles slyly to himself. Is he the only one to pick up what I have just said?

But wait. The VC turns to the Director of Human Resources next to him. In a stagy way he raises his eyebrows at him. It seems another contribution is about to be made.

"Ah yes. Professor Grylls? Do you have any questions for this interview panel?"

"If I were to be offered this post, when would you want my answer by?"

The VC intervenes.

"I don't like those who hedge their bets. That question comes across as a little devious to me."

I am quite taken aback. I feel annoyed by his rude remark.

HR man tries to step in as best he can.

"Do you have any more questions, Professor Grylls?"

I cannot help myself. To hell with it. Here goes.

"This and other art schools now making up the Institute were previously under the Inner London Education Authority – as primary and secondary schools still are, I believe?"

"Yes."

"And the principal of each college, like the head of a primary or secondary school, was responsible for the academic as well as the managerial leadership of their college?"

The VC senses a challenge. He takes over.

"What are you asking?"

"Well, I was in America when this Institute was set up. So I don't know much about the philosophy of organisation here. I was just trying to establish whether the Vice-Chancellor is the academic as well as the managerial leader of the Institute, or are the heads of the colleges still autonomous academic leaders – based, of course, on their professional knowledge of the art and design world?"

"Carry on," scowls the VC.

"I'm sorry if I'm not being clear. I'll try and put it simply, if a bit crudely. Is the role of Vice-Chancellor here equivalent to that of a traditional Vice-Chancellor – responsible for the academic as well as managerial leadership of a university – or to that of a Chief Education Officer in a local authority who would only intervene if something disastrous happened, the way things were before the Institute was set up?"

M & S Bob is bobbing from me to the VC and back as though he is enjoying an exciting tennis tournament.

"I, as Vice-Chancellor, lead firmly here. Academically, managerially. You name it."

"Okay. So, as they are all art and design colleges making up the Institute, what is your own professional art and design experience?"

"I do not have any. I do not need any. I have substantial leadership experience."

"But how can you lead four or is it five college heads, each of whom will have their own ideas for where their college should go, without being experienced and qualified in art and design yourself? Who will be responsible for the University adding up to more than its constituent parts? It can't be the VC, if the VC is not an art and design academic. Can it? I am not trying to be personal."

"I do not like your tone. What is your real agenda in pursuing this?"

"Sorry. I don't have an agenda. You asked me if I had any questions – or rather he did. It is simply that I take this post seriously and the answers will help me decide whether of not to accept – assuming, of course, I was offered this post."

"It will not be necessary for me to answer that, Vaughan, because, in view of what you have just said and your general attitude, you will not be offered this post. "

The VC leans back in his chair grimacing. A now clearly nonplussed M & S man continues looking from me to the VC and back again. HR man gets up, eyes ready to pop, rounds the table and escorts me to the door. The governor remains seated, silent, non-contributing. Is he stuffed? He would not be the only one, had I been offered this job and accepted it.

In the few years that I had been away, the whole tenor of higher education in England had changed. Although the established universities at first resisted Thatcherism, the new "independent" higher education institutions and polytechnics were now eager, indeed desperate, to follow the government's bidding.

WALSALL POLYTECHNIC, 1989

The Polytechnic was assembled, starting in 1969, by joining the art college (where I had once been a student, 1964–67), the technical college and a teacher training college. Unlike the established universities, there was no shared ethos even by 1989, other than one imposed from the top. This consisted of a totalitarian disregard for anything deemed bourgeois or elitist, excepting, of course, large salaries and titles awarded to senior staff. I was thinking of joining them.

"Here is your room, Professor Grylls. You're booked in for two nights, like all the candidates."

"Well, I don't know whether I'll be here for both nights. Who are you?"

"I'm Gordon, sir. Gordon Staple. Senior Porter at what was not long ago Brownhills College of Education."

"Pleased to meet you, Gordon. What I meant was, I don't know how long I'll be here. That really depends on what happens tomorrow."

"Oh, but we have all the candidates down for two nights."

"Well, the thing is, the interview invitation says they will only want to keep selected candidates for a second round of interviews on day two. I may not be one of them."

"Didn't know that. But then they don't tell us anything about anything down here, do they? We're now the poor relations down here, sir."

"Oh. Communications not too good at the Poly, Gordon?"

"Communications sir? Don't make me laugh. Sorry. Shouldn't have said that. You're all here for the Head of the School of Art & Design job, aren't you? They did tell us that."

"That's right. How many candidates are here, Gordon? I haven't seen anyone around."

"They're all tucked up in bed, sir. At least I assume they are. Nine, including you."

"Nine? That is quite a bunch. Yes, sorry I'm the last. I did let them know I would be here very late. But thank you for waiting up. I've come quite a long way, Gordon."

"No problem, Professor Grylls. We were told to expect you late. They do tell us some things."

"Well, it is nearly midnight. And I have to be at the main Polytechnic building by nine o'clock tomorrow. But, just one thing . . . tell me . . . is this college a full part of the Polytechnic now?"

"It is, sir. They took us over. Couple of years ago now. Lovely college we were. Training teachers. Half the staff have gone. Frightened off out, they were. A lot had been here for donkey's years."

"That sounds very sad. Couldn't they take the new style, Gordon?"

"Style, sir? They were brutes. Me? I'd chuck it in if I could afford to, sir. The worst was what they did to the Principal. Lovely man he was. We all respected him. He knew everyone. Had a word for us all – the staff, us, the students. Lovely man."

"What happened?"

"Happened? I'll tell you what happened, sir! One day, that Dr Dannage and another fellow, Mr Blidworth I think it was, came down from the Poly to see him and the next day he had a heart attack. It was a big one. Did for him, it did. Died that weekend. God rest his soul. Anyway, sir, I've said too much. Breakfast tomorrow from seven o'clock. By the way, sir, I have been asked to give you this."

Gordon hands me an envelope.

"Good night, sir. Sleep well."

"Good night, Gordon. And thank you for waiting up."

"It's a pleasure, Professor. You're a gentleman."

He is gone. I open the envelope.

Please deliver a ten-minute presentation tomorrow entitled:

"What are the key issues facing the School of Art & Design and, as Head of School, how will you address them?"

Presentation time:

V. Grylls. 12 noon. School of Engineering Lecture Theatre.

That topic was included in the letter inviting me for interview, but now I have my time slot.

"It is nine a.m. and here we all are. You'll each be expected to give a presentation, as you know. So be here fifteen minutes before the time of your presentation. Rest of the time, you'll be given a tour of the School of Art & Design. And then be back here by six p.m. Any questions?"

He is tall and thin, wearing a light-cream suit, winklepickers and a loud tie, and is drawing on a cigarette.

Before I ask, another candidate does it for me.

"Could we ask . . . who you are?"

"Yeah, sure. I'm Pete. Pete Stepney, Director of the Polytechnic. So. As I was saying. You'll be divided into groups of three. A B and C. To be shown round."

We are left to introduce one another. In my group is Marilyn, Head of Three-Dimensional Design at the Polytechnic in Sheffield, and Gerald, Vice-Principal of some art college in the Welsh Marches. We wait for our allotted guide. I kick off the small talk.

"So why do you want to come here, Gerald? Being a Vice-Principal already."

"Because my college is being closed and all the degree courses are being transferred here to the School of Art & Design at the end of this academic year. And I'm the Vice-Principal responsible for those degree and higher diploma courses."

"But are not you being transferred with them?"

"That is still a subject of intense debate. But at the highest level. Between the County Education Authority and the senior Directorate here. "

"Oh."

"Ay oop. I'm Fred. Fred Dannage. I've got to show you boggers round."

A man in his late fifties with an exaggerated northern accent has just introduced himself, kitted out as Fidel Castro sans beard. Dannage? Haven't I heard that name before?

"Hello, Fred. I'm Vaughan, this is Marilyn and this is Gerald."

"I know who he is all right."

Fred smirks as I remember. That fatal heart attack.

"Follow me then. Over to the School of Art & Design. We'll start in my office."

Off we traipse, down a path, round a corner and there in front of us rises the School of Art & Design.

"Come on. This way."

Why does this revolutionary figure, leading us, have his office there? I wonder what he does in Art & Design. I have never heard of him.

"Fred?"

"Yeah?"

"What is your own Art & Design discipline? Just wondered . . . as a matter of interest."

We are about to enter the building. He stops in his tracks. So we all stop. He turns.

"What makes you think I've got one?"

"Just that you said we were going to your office."

"I know fuck all about Art & Design. I'm a quantity surveyor." That smirk again.

We are now in the entrance hall heading for the lift. In we get and stand in silence. A student gets in on floor three and out at five. We reach the seventh, head past the Painting studios towards what is presumably Fred's office. Into a reception area which has three large framed prints. It is difficult to recognise who they are by, but I manage. They are the work of a staff member at the Royal College of Art who, like me, was once a student here. It is difficult to see them because they now have a different function – notice boards with notes stuck all over them. This is appalling. What am I doing here? Into Fred's den we go. Full-length windows. The view of the distant countryside is astonishing. Below, a panorama of the town laid out at our feet. As for the room itself, well, it would be difficult to furnish more grimly than this – lots of old filing cabinets, piles of curling papers on battered desks, collapsing and filthy Venetian blinds stuck back with masking tape. Fred's office looks as though it could be in *The Spy Who Came in from the Cold*. But in the corner are two expensive Bauhaus-style leather armchairs – Breuer, I think. Left over from a previous era when the Principal of the Art College's office was expected to have some sense of design?

"Find somewhere to sit . . . if you can. I'll stand." says Fred.

"Vaughan . . . it is Vaughan, isn't it? . . . wonders why I'm here. I'll tell you why I'm here. I'm the Dean of the Arts Faculty of which the School of Art & Design is now a part. I'm a quantity surveyor, though. So I don't know about English or Art History or Sociology either. They are over at a recently acquired campus. We moved them over there when we closed down that teacher training they did. What I do know about is running a budget. And the Faculty of Art & Design was over-funded for years. Over-funded! So, when Pete came – the Director, that is – him and me and Norman Blidworth, who is the Deputy Director, had to get hold of all this shit so what we did was demote Art & Design from being a Faculty in its own right, shift its Art History out and that has given room to get in the courses which Gerald here has been in charge of. Isn't that right, Gerald?"

Gerald looks sheepishly smily. He nods. Marilyn's mouth has dropped quite a bit. I don't know what I look like – probably a combination of the two. Fred lights a cigarette. He is clearly savouring the moment.

"Any questions? You can have a wander round. Meet me at the entrance at eleven-thirty. I'll then show you the lecture theatre. Whether there's a lecture in there or not."

"Is there a Head of the Art & Design School now?" asks Marilyn.

"Acting. Just acting."

"I see. Will we be able to meet him or her?"

"He's one of the candidates." This news is something additional for Fred to savour. He clearly relishes the discomforture of others.

We leave Fred's office to wander round. I hang back in the reception, pretending to admire the disfigured prints. I need to catch Fred alone.

"Fred?"

"Yes, Vaughan?"

"What is the one thing you think the School of Art & Design needs to do to help the Polytechnic?"

"Get off its arse."

"To do what?"

"Offer something to the Poly! Instead of basking in its application rates."

"Are the application rates higher here than in the rest of the Poly?"

"Yeah. You bet they are."

"And where are they lowest? In subjects like Engineering? And Languages?"

"Yeah."

"So they could help by developing joint courses – Three-Dimensional Design with Engineering say? That sort of thing."

"Fooking right."

"Thanks."

I'm not going to waste precious time looking around at students in studios. The main thing is I know some of the staff who are still here. They taught me. I need to pick two or three off and get the lowdown from them. Find one, ask him to take me to a quiet room that the other candidates won't go in, and then phone up one or two other staff from my time here and get them to join us. I'll then find a bog, lock myself in and adapt my crib sheet. And then I'll meet Fred downstairs at eleven-thirty. I've got two hours max.

"God, Vaughan. It is great to see you here. It has been hell, the last two years. Andrew Dainton, the Dean of Art & Design, had to take early retirement. Then Dr Fred Dannage came in. Then Mark. Mark Baxter, you know, Head of Ceramics. They made him Head of School under Fred. Then he retired as he couldn't deal with Fred. And then I went to see Fred to suggest Mark be given an Honorary Fellowship as he'd been here thirty-five years and he told me to 'piss off out of his office'. Awful it was."

"I'm sorry to hear that, Guy. Bad manners."

"Manners, Vaughan? Manners? That's the last thing these people have."

"Look. Guy, Keith, Patrick. I know you want to get all this off your chest, but I have to give a presentation in just over an hour. What is the one thing you would like to see done? And don't say 'take the Art college out of the Polytechnic', even though I know that would be the ideal. It cannot be done. Sorry."

"Get them off our back."

"You would have to set up some joint courses with deadbeat schools over there. If it is controlled, it is a price worth paying."

"Could be the thin end of the wedge, Vaughan."

"You are right. But the alternative would be worse. An imposed settlement. You see, handled deftly, those deadbeat schools could become dependent on this place."

"It is risky, Vaughan."

"Tell me about it. Look. I've got to go."

"Vaughan. Good luck."

"Well, this is the Art & Design Lecture Theatre. This should be bookable by the whole Poly. It isn't yet. Let's go in."

Fred pushes at the door. A slide lecture is taking place. Chinese ceramics.

"Hello. Just want to show this place to these candidates."

The lecturer is on the podium. Fred does not bother to introduce us to her. Instead he waves us in and walking to the front, places himself between the lecturer and her students.

"These are some of our Art & Design students," says Fred. And then, turning to us, "These are some of the candidates for the Head of School post we are interviewing for."

A disembodied voice calls from the gloom at the back.

"Who are you?"

"We'll try and rally a few more takers, Mr Grylls. Don't know where everyone is this morning. It was well advertised."

"Well, this is the office number I scribbled down of one of the staff in Art & Design. You could try that. They may be able to rustle some up. What about Engineering?"

"Oh, yes. Thanks."

The HR manager disappears. Will she bring more in? I'm due to start in ten minutes. There are about half a dozen in the audience so far.

I've decided not to show slides. I"ll use instead the one-sheet prompt page I finished rewriting in the loo not so long ago. Also, if it is dark, as it has to be with projectors, I can't read the audience's reaction. Anyway, there won't be many to see the reaction of.

End with fifteen takers, including the Director, Fred Dannage, Norman Blidworth, the Head of Engineering, whom I chat with afterwards – nice guy – and the three old-timers I had organised that surreptitious meeting with. There is also a Dr Lionel Power, a pompous man who wishes to impress on me when it comes to question time his four credentials – Dean of the Business School, a member of Directorate, that he will be on the main interview panel tomorrow, and that he is conversant with American universities where he has just spent a week "researching their approach to modularity".

Six p.m. and now we are eight applicants – one having withdrawn – awaiting the arrival of the Director. The door opens. Here he is. Pete Stepney. With entourage.

"Okay, ladies and gentlemen. So. Let's see."

The HR manager hands him a sheet of paper.

"Thanks, darling. So. Here we have it . . . Gorman, Sadley, Jennings, Smith-Robertson, Keble. Can you please come over here? Cheers everyone."

That's it, then. The Director and co. have made their first selection. Disappointment followed by a sense of relief. Not to worry. I have a job of sorts which I eventually managed to get not long after leaving America. I'm running general photography courses at Oxford Polytechnic. Doesn't pay much, especially in comparison to my American salary, but it's better than nothing. And then, as I'm pulling on my overcoat . . .

"You lot can go now. We won't want to see you any more. Bye."

Well, thanks for rubbing it in, Pete.

As I reach the door, the HR manager heads me off.

"He doesn't mean you, Mr Grylls. Those were the candidates who did not get through the first filter. We want to see you and two other candidates tomorrow for the formal interview. Ten a.m. Council Room."

"Evening, Gordon."

"Evening, sir. You're with us for another day then?"

"Appears so. To be honest, I'm amazed. Don't know whether I should stay or go."

"Well, look. It's dark and foggy. You may as well stay the night anyway, sir, and sleep on it. If you just want a pint and a sandwich, there's a quiet pub just five minutes away. I can direct you, if you're interested."

"Thanks, Gordon. Perfect. Where is it?"

It's ten past ten in the morning and I'm still sitting outside the Polytechnic's Council Room. The other two candidates not around. Now feel a bit worried. Why am I here? Let's see. Sorry for my old college and staff? Maybe. Need more money coming in? Definitely. Think you could get on with the new bosses? Don't make me laugh . . . oh dear, here she comes. The HR manager.

"Morning, Mr Grylls. I've just had a phone call from the Director and he says they are ready for you. Sorry they are running a bit late. You can go straight in to the Council Room."

In I go. First is the view through the windows. There, in the unexpected sunshine, is the original art college building where once I was interviewed for a place as a student. Now I scan the council room of the old tech college, big and designed to impress, which it does. At its far end, under large portraits of past chairmen of governors and principals of the technical college, has been placed a long oak table. Four men sit in a line behind the table, each togged up in slick double-breasted business suits. Their suits look nothing like the lived-in suits with their crumpled waistcoats and watch-chains depicted in the portraits above. The most astonishing transformation is to Fred Dannage. He's exchanged Che Guevara for Gordon Gecko. So what. We're all playing a part here and I know where I have to sit. And this is the court martial scene from *Mutiny on the Bounty* with me as Lieutenant Bligh, for in the middle of the room stands the hot seat – a modest metal chair. Must have been released from that stack on the left.

Pete Stepney waves me to it.

"Come in, Vaughan. That's right. You met everyone yesterday. Well. Let's get started. You first looked out the window when you came in. What were you thinking about?"

Pete has taken me off guard from the beginning. Astute.

"Oh, sorry. Just that I was interviewed over there as a student, twenty-odd years ago. When the art college was a separate institution."

Norman Blidworth, Deputy Director: "They would still like to be."

"They still have been, in all but name. Until we got hold of them quite recently." Fred Dannage.

Norman ignores Fred. "They say they are the jewel in the crown of the Polytechnic. What do you say, Mr Grylls?"

"Well . . . I would think . . . A crown and a polytechnic are strange bedfellows."

Pete Stepney cackles.

"Seriously, though. Are they that good?"

"They are, actually. A very sound reputation. When I was a student they were known for teaching high-quality technical skills as well as encouraging original ideas. Not very philosophical like some of the London art schools and places like Bath Academy of Art, but very practical. They used to refer to your artwork as your "job". Fine Art as well as Design. A past President of the Royal Academy was trained here as was the current Professor of Sculpture at the Royal College of Art and the Professor of Printmaking there. Dr Dannage has some of his impressive work hanging outside his office. He would know whom I'm referring to." (Had to throw that one in.)

I look at Pete Stepney in the middle. The others are unpleasant, lesser men. I have to convince him. If I want the job, that is. Not sure, but at least that means I can afford to be relaxed. I'll take the bull by the horns.

"Director . . ."

"Yes, Vaughan. Oh, and just call me Pete."

"Pete. You want the Art School to integrate better with the Poly. And the staff there don't want to, if they can help it? Yes?"

"You know that, Vaughan. Seeing you've had a secret pow-wow with some of the staff over there yesterday."

He's managed to backfoot me again. Sharp.

"Yes. How did you know?"

"We have our spies. Here and there. Anyway, I'd expect you to. Seeing as you know some of them of old. Do you know, they told me you are one of their star turns. That's why you're here."

He has given me a riposte opportunity. Deliberately. Obviously likes a bit of banter. Not like the bozos he's surrounded himself with. That bit worries me most of all about this job.

I laugh. "Star turn. So you do take on board some of their views!"

Norman Blidworth interrupts. "Not when they are non-communicative, actively obstructive and even . . ."

Pete waves him to be quiet. "Yeah, yeah, Norman. Let's find a way through this. Let's get to the point. What can you bring here, Vaughan, if we offer you this job?"

"Well. As I touched on yesterday in my presentation, I think I would start by setting up special pilot degree courses, joint honours, say, between the art school and certain schools in the Poly, with recruitment challenges – Engineering? I think I got on well with the head of school when I had a chat with him afterwards – see how those go, learn from them but also keep the traditional Art School courses going alongside. After all, those attract good overseas student income, I understand, so there is little point in an own-goal, damaging the income they generate. So evolution, not revolution, to produce what I think would benefit the Polytechnic in the longer term."

Norman comes in again. "Dr Dannage has put that sort of thing to them until he's blue in the face. Right, Fred?"

Fred does his smirk and nods.

I'll be bold.

"With due respect to Dr Dannage – a quantity surveyor, right? – that was him. This is me – one of their former art and design students, their 'star turn' – who has been out in the world, been successful, knows the world has changed. They haven't. Of course they want to hold on entirely to what has worked in the past. But, as you know, the past gets further and further away every day. So you have to change. Just to stay still. At least incrementally. I think they'll listen to me."

"Star turn?"

"Yes, Pete. The star turn factor could be the key to cooperation."

Pete turns to the Business Director. The pompous Lionel Power. "Lionel?"

"We are looking for greater integration than a few courses being set up. We are introducing a completely porous modular system throughout the Polytechnic. Students will be able to take anything with anything."

"Oh, good. This is the system informed by your visit to America?

The one you told me about yesterday."

"That is it."

"You went over for a week, did you say?"

"Yep."

Pete cackles. He has given me the green light to be bold again.

"I was over there four years. And all US universities pretty much offer what we call modular systems and they call courses. I taught at an East Coast university, as you know, but I was also a regular visiting professor at Washington University in St Louis, the University of Wisconsin and the University of South Dakota. So two private and two state universities. And they all run complex systems. With prerequisites, corequisites and different rules according to the year of study in question, and the subjects involved. They have been in development since the end of the Second World War. They are sophisticated with high set-up and maintenance costs. But that is the price of operating a coherent consumer-led system in the most consumer-led country in the world. But it is not a free-for all. Not in the good universities, anyway."

Fred weighs in. "But that is just what we want. Pick and mix for students with low A levels. We want to give students the real power. Not the staff. And all I want to know is . . ."

Pete cuts across. "Yeah, but that is interesting what Vaughan says about modularity. So let's turn to costs. The art school say we've cut their costs too hard. They were used to living high on the hog. Much better funded than any other faculty. For years."

I pause. How shall I respond to this?

"Since the Polytechnic was set up, I should think. The Art College was always better funded than the Technical College, I would have thought. It was the local education authority's star turn. Anyway, all I am saying is that today what was once called the Art College . . ."

Norman interrupts. "We call it E block now."

Pete interrupts him in return.

"Yeah, well, as I was saying, Vaughan, that is an expensive building to run. So what the fuck do we do?"

Did he say "fuck"? I haven't heard swear words in an interview since that bogus one with Kevin Crumb in 1983.

"I'm not surprised, Pete. I remember when it was built. Money no object. And state-of-the-art equipped back then. Local politicians always love big thing – a-me-jigs, of course. Political stepping stones for them. But they don't think about the maintenance costs, year in, year out. They never have to. Their careers have moved on. The art college was no exception."

"Yeah. That is a shrewd observation, Vaughan. So what would you do now?"

"Er . . . work out how much it will cost to get repaired. To a basic level. And then spread those repairs over a number of years. Urgent first, of course. And separately, work out a maintenance schedule and cost that out also. Then hypothecate the overseas student income and apply it just to the maintenance costs. Urgent repairs would probably have to be funded centrally. I would need to see the figures. It won't be easy, of course."

Pete now leans back and strokes his chin. The three bozos look at him silently. He leans forward, so I do the same.

"What alternatives are there? One of the candidates suggested we could sell off some of the Art & Design collection. Like those pictures you mentioned. That would raise a bit."

"Marginal. Like selling some of the family silver. You need a proper, structured funding plan. As for alternatives, you could close it down, which would definitely be an own goal, or sell it as a going concern – although the government may not allow that. So I don't think there is a credible alternative to what I've suggested."

"Does education have to take place in high-quality state-of-the-art premises for it to be good, Vaughan?"

"Not really. The day before yesterday I was staying the night at Exeter College, Oxford. My brother teaches at Oxford. The room I was in was cold, with just a one-bar electric fire, and it was falling apart in places – probably been like that for the past three hundred years – and there was no toilet nearby for a night visit, other than directly out of the window into the Rector's garden. But no one gives a damn about all that. Oxford is Oxford, you see."

Ha, ha ha! Pete likes this.

"So did you use the garden?"

"I'm not saying, Pete."

"You did. I know you did! So, I think that's all. Do you have any further questions?"

"Not really. Other than when will you make a decision? As for the Art College – sorry, E block – please don't despair. I'm confident it can be sorted."

"We'll make a decision today, Vaughan. And convey it tonight or tomorrow. Leave your phone number with HR. Where will you be?"

"Actually I'm off to stay with an old friend. He has a place near Gladestry in Wales. It's a converted pig-sty in the middle of nowhere, although I think converted is probably too fanciful a description. So I'll be staying at the Royal Oak down there."

Pete stands and walks round the table. He shakes my hand. The others remain seated, which is good. I don't really want to shake their hands.

"Thanks for attending, Vaughan. Enjoy Wales. If not the pig-sty."

The landlord shouts across to where I'm playing pool with John.

"Vaughan Grylls? Phone call."

"Hello?"

"Vaughan?"

"Yes."

It's Pete Stepney, Vaughan. We'd like to offer you Head of the School of Art & Design. Will you accept?"

"Oh, thanks, Pete. In principle, yes. But can I come and see you as soon as possible?"

"Sure. Tomorrow?"

"It's Saturday tomorrow."

"Yeah, come to my house. Got a pen? Here is the address. One o'clock? I'll get an Indian takeaway. Do you like them? My wife likes them."

I return to the pool table.

"John?"

"Yeah?"

"That's the first job I've been offered in a pub. Let's get another round in."

I ran an art school of which I was proud and which developed a strong in-ternational reputation. But in my seven years there, I spent far too much time deflecting, by fair means or foul, Norman Blidworth and co.'s further assaults on the Art School. These could be vicious, petty or just plain ill-mannered, but at least they were sporadic and unintelligent and you didn't have to use too much brain-power to deflect them.

There was another factor. The government relaxed the cap on stu-dent numbers, which meant that the art school, which had less than four hundred students when I arrived, had over a thousand when I left and was operating on more or less the same resource base. Some of the expansion was due to the transfer of the courses from other colleges. Expansion was the name of the game throughout the whole polytechnic sector, irrespective of discipline.

Although difficult to manage, the ability to expand, due to the best application rates in the Polytechnic by a long shot, did give us political lever-age, and that meant we could turn a problem into an opportunity, as I'd figured out before my interview.

In the early nineties, the government suddenly allowed polytechnics to re-badge themselves as universities. Everyone was ecstatic, except the Art School which didn't really care. We were well known anyway, university title or not. Perhaps it was best summed up by a cabby at the train station in my last week.

"The University's School of Art & Design, please."

"Do yow mean the Art College?"

EDINBURGH COLLEGE OF ART, 1990

Taxpayers' funding for university students was much higher in Scotland than in England and Wales. Added to that, Scottish universities and colleges were not obliged to expand student places at the new, heavily reduced price per student. So when the Principalship at Edinburgh College of Art became vacant, I applied at once. Perhaps I was selected for interview because they thought my name sounded non-Anglo.

Before my interview, I conducted an interview myself with an old acquaintance – the mercurial midwife of the Edinburgh Festival, Edinburgh gallery director, Richard Demarco.

"It's great to see you up here, Vaughan! Did you take the train?"

"No, I drove up, Ricky. I wanted to stop off at Hadrian's Wall to visit once more where I made that work just before I went to the US."

"Ah, yes. The one Polaroid commissioned. I remember. A polaroid of each stone in the wall joined together."

"Well, not the whole wall, Ricky. Just a couple of yards of it."

"They should have paid for the whole wall in polaroids. Although you'd still be down there now."

"Indeed. So, what about the art college here. Am I doing the right thing?"

"Yes, of course. It would be great if you got the job. But don't frighten the horses. And don't, don't, under any circumstances, say you've seen me."

"Oh? Why not?"

"They hate me."

"Why?"

"Why? Because I've drawn attention to their conservatism too many times. Publicly."

"I see. Not exactly Edinburgh Fringe over there."

"You can say that, all right. A place where time has stood still. It needs a kick up the arse."

"It has some famous alumni. And a solid reputation."

"Yeah. Too solid. Hasn't moved. For a long time. And doesn't want to, Vaughan. You'll see."

"I'm Dr Declan McLeod, welcome to the Caledonian Hotel. All six candidates appear to be here. So now, this evening we'll take a few drinks and nibbles and then at seven p.m. repair for a buffet supper next door. This will be a chance for you to chat informally with our various members of the Board of Governors and also, of course, with one another."

I scan the room. We, the candidates are grouped near the door. We are all men. Four are in suits, I'm in a sports jacket from Bloomingdales, New York – the one I wore for that interview at Walsall – and there is one candidate in a kilt. And he has a big beard. Could be Queen Victoria's ghilly.

The mingling starts and before I can introduce myself to the nearest person, Dr McLeod slides over to me.

"I see you are Professor Vaughan Grylls."

A smart Edinburgh accent.

I glance down at my badge.

"Yes, it appears I am. And you, I see, are Dr Declan McLeod, Chairman of Governors. I am very pleased to meet you. And thank you so much for calling me for interview."

A cocktail waitress hovers. The Chairman waves her away.

"Don't mention it, Professor Grylls. It is a pleasure."

A pause, and then, "So. When did you arrive in Edinburgh?"

"Early this afternoon."

"And how have you been filling your time?"

"Well, I've been pretty busy. I visited an old friend in Edinburgh, drove to my hotel, checked in, and I then went over to spend too little time at the Scottish National Gallery."

"Had you been before?"

"As a matter of fact, yes. Just a couple of years ago."

"Yes. You must have noticed the changes."

"I did. It looks so much better now."

"Oh, yes. In what way particularly?"

"Well, they've restored the gallery to its original Victorian glory, as they call it. All those white cubicles and false ceilings have been stripped out."

"Better now?"

"Er, well, yes."

I sense danger but can only plough on. "I think the restoration shows off the historic collection more sympathetically."

"I see. Why do you think it does that?"

"Well, they were never meant to be hung on brilliant white Dulux walls. Wouldn't you agree?"

"Actually, Professor Grylls, I wouldn't agree. I'm afraid I was the previous director, you see. And I installed those, what did you call them, Dulux walls?"

"Well, I'm sorry but . . ."

"No, no. Please do not concern yourself. You are entitled to your opinion. Oh, look. Over there is Lady Raith. Let me introduce you."

Seven p.m. A second man in a kilt enters carrying a large bell. He throws open the large double doors at the end of the room and rings it.

"My lords, ladies and gentlemen. Your buffet supper is now served. Please make your way, at your convenience, through to the dining room. Thank you."

"Unusual to start with the *plat principal* at a buffet?"

I turn round. The Chair of Governors is standing at my elbow. Wrong-footed again.

"Ah, yes. I decided to skip the *hors d'oeuvre*. I had too much lunch, I'm afraid, Dr McLeod."

"I see. Well, you do seem to cram things in, Professor Grylls. Visiting a friend, large lunch and then a bit of the National Gallery. Shame you are having to pass over the *entrée* as well. It is very good."

He gestures at his plate. I feel like pushing mine in his face and walking out. I am not bold enough. I just counter.

"It is all very good, it appears. Spoilt for choice as they say. Well, it should be. Edinburgh College of Art is very good. So I suppose this whole buffet-interview is a fitting, er, *hors d'oeuvre* to the main course tomorrow?"

"Ah, excellent. Tell me. I was interested in your application and curriculum vitae. From an Ivy League New England college to a Midlands polytechnic! Quite a, how shall I say . . . range? Very different experiences? So, what would you say is the one most important responsibility of a college principal? Sorry to jump that one on you before you delve into . . ."

"The main course?"

"Touché."

"Advancing the academic standards while remaining solvent."

"H'mm. Not being the principal ambassador? We'll have to agree to disagree on that! Anyway, tonight is a social occasion. So I look forward to seeing you tomorrow at your interview at the College."

The six candidates are sitting having afternoon tea in our hotel just off Gordon Square. We've been interviewed and now we are awaiting a telephone call to the hotel for one of us to return to be offered the Principalship.

"Professor O'Brien?"

The Irish guy turns.

"Yes?"

"Could you follow me, please. You have a phone call."

He gets up, bows to the rest of us and, wearing his kilt, heads for the door.

Edinburgh College of Art lost its independence many years later and is now a college of the University of Edinburgh.

THE PRATT INSTITUTE, NEW YORK, 1990

In 1989 I married a New Yorker and it was she who first saw the advertisement in the New York Times *placed by mid-town Manhattan headhunters for a new Dean of Art & Design at The Pratt Institute in Brooklyn, New York. The Pratt Institute has, according to* USA Today, *the best art and design school in America. I posted a letter of application and, a week or so later, I was invited to New York. There I had a brief conversation with one head-hunting man. It seemed a long way to go for such a short and informal discussion but a few days after that, by which time I was back in England, he rang to say I had been placed on their longlist of nine candidates and could I come over for a formal interview at the Pratt Institute at their expense in two weeks' time? So back I flew, but it wasn't really a formal interview, more a question and answer presentation by me of my art works to an audience of faculty and students. After that, I bid farewell to my new wife, who was working in New York, and yet again flew back to England, thinking I would not hear from them again. But I was wrong.*

"These seats are pretty tight. These are not first-class seats."

I turn to my companion. Middle-aged American businessman. Balding. Munching nuts.

"Really? I've never sat in a first class seat."

"Yeah, really. Well, you've paid for the one you're sitting in right now. Or someone has."

I glance out the window. The earth is curved at this height. Extraordinary. I cannot believe I am here. And now I have thought of a riposte.

"Well, your tight seat is just the bad news. The good news is you don't have to sit in it for long."

He laughs. The nuts are about to spill out.

"I guess you are right, my friend. But from now on it is back to first class on a British Airways 747 for me. I'd rather have my fat ass on one of their seats for seven and a half hours than have it sat for three and a half hours on their goddam Concorde."

Riverside Drive, Manhattan.

"It is only for tonight. I have to return to London tomorrow."

"Sure, Vaughan. You can stay here at my mother's apartment. So you and your new wife are estranged already?"

"You could say that, John."

"You're not very good at interviewing women for a wife position, are you, Vaughan?"

"You could also say that, John."

"Huh. Well, anyway, I thought you wanted a job in England so you could see your daughter? And then you got one over there. It is great to see you, but why come back again?"

"Because she saw the ad. And I'm over there all right but I should have stayed at that job at Oxford Polytechnic. But it didn't pay enough to pay maintenance. You know. Anyway, the thing is, I've just got to get out. Some of those people are oafs. I should not have taken the job. It was stupid."

"I'm sorry to hear that."

"Yes, well. I tried a job in Scotland, you know, but that didn't work. So now I'm back here."

"Yeah. In a city with someone you shouldn't have married. Tell me again why did you marry her. I still can't believe the story."

"Well, I pulled out at the last moment, as you know. And then I decided to go ahead as my mother said the tension was giving her diarrhoea."

" I just love it. The first and only time diarrhoea has been cited as the reason for marriage."

"Yes, well, there you are, John. And here I am. It's all a mess, I know."

"A diarrhoea of a mess, Vaughan. Tell me, where did you get that suit?"

"My soon to be ex-wife bought it. For our marriage last year."

"Did she indeed? Well, I hope you're not wearing it to your interview tomorrow morning."

"Oh, why? That was the intention."

"You're crazy. They are looking to hire a tweedy English guy. Not a croupier from Atlantic City. You'll never get the job in that."

"Well, maybe I don't want the job. Maybe I don't know what I want."

Pratt Institute, Brooklyn New York.

"Well, it is just great to see you back, Professor Grylls, as one of our two final candidates. It's been quite a haul for you but I trust we made it a little easier. How did that work out?"

"Very well. Although I was taken aback when the agency advised me to hop the Concorde."

"But here you are. Our apologies to have given such short notice, Professor Grylls. Today was the only day we could get a quorum of Trustees. The alternative was another month."

I am sitting at the end of a long polished table, at the far end of which is the Chair of Trustees and to his left the President of the Pratt Institute. On the table's left flank sit two women; on the right, two men. All Trustees. I know as there are name plates in front of each of them. The Chair has been speaking. He turns to the President.

"Ted, you want to start?"

"Yeah, sure. Vaughan, could I call you that?"

"Of course."

"Vaughan, when you were last here, you explained about two deputies you have, both of whom are constantly looking for perquisites. I just loved that story. Could you tell it again? For those of us who were not here last time?"

"Yes, as you may remember, they had both applied for the job I now have. Since I arrived one badgered me constantly for a professorship, the other for a professorship one week, a designated parking space the next. So I told that guy that, although neither is in my gift, at this polytechnic, although it is difficult to get a professorship, it is almost impossible to get a dedicated parking space. It was my greatest academic honour to have one."

"Ha! I just love that. Don't you just love that?"

He glances round the table. Smiles all round, some forced. Oh dear. The forced ones are not from Trustees. They are from professors. Damn. I thought they were all Trustees.

"Er, of course, a professorship in the UK is an awarded title and is not used as a courtesy title for all university faculty as here. So, er, it would not apply here . . ."

"Yes, we are aware of that, Vaughan. But it makes a good story, doesn't it? So, just one more of those. The story about the guy you had to make redundant?"

"Oh, yes. It was a few years ago now. My mother inherited a small family company in Nottingham and she asked me to help her out. The bank said they were about to foreclose on the company when she inherited it. As part of the new business plan I had to restructure, which meant letting the old sales manager go. He took us to court and argued that he was the most important and highly paid member of staff and therefore should be the last one to be declared redundant. So I said to the tribunal that it was true what he said but the fact that we had to let someone of his status go indicated what a serious financial situation the company faced. We were heartbroken to have to do it."

"And they bought it?"

"Technically no, but in reality yes, as they awarded a token sum in damages."

"A few bucks."

"Yes. Very few."

The Chair and President smile as do the other two Trustees. But the Head of Graphic Design and the Head of Visual Arts are now scowling at these appalling boss tales from a guy looking like a – what was it? – oh yes, an Atlantic City croupier.

A woman Trustee weighs in.

"These are great tales, Vaughan. But I think your work is greater. I loved your presentation last time. Those murals, *Site of the Kennedy Assassination* and the other, er, the British Museum one, well, how did they play with liberal arts students? Those students they take at Massachusetts College are pretty bright."

"Yes. They are. About the highest SAT entry scores in America. I found that, in general terms, my students who were art majors warmed to my work but those students who were doing a double major, especially art and economics or art and political science, warmed even more. Indeed, once or twice I had to deflect those students from the path of imitation."

"It touched several bases for them because of the content. Your work isn't just about art things."

"I guess not. Maybe I should have been an historian or something, instead of an artist."

"Well, I for one am pleased you're not. I get kinda sick of this shallow, blown-up bullshit over here. We now have graffiti art, you know."

The Chair interrupts. "Sally, I think that is a great point. But may I bring Beatrice in? Beatrice, I know you want to explore another perspective with Vaughan."

"Thank you. But first can I pick up on something – a thread – in your resumé here. Most of the people we've looked at for the position of Dean of our art school, well, their experience is just teaching in other art schools. But from this, okay, you did that early on, but then you were teaching art teachers – to teach, I guess, Cambridge and er . . ."

I nod.

"That is true. But they had to continue making their own art. I felt that to be fundamental – practically and philosophically, morally even."

Beatrice nods back. "Sure, I can see that. But then you came to the States to teach in a top liberal arts college where students don't necessarily go to learn to be artists, or designers, you know. Why did you choose to work in non-mainstream art environments?"

"Well, I'm working in one now – in fact I'm running one. But, to answer your question as succinctly as possible. I've always been interested as much in the world outside the art world as the world inside the art world. Perhaps more so. Not to sound too grand, but what can art do to address the world in general and the people in it?"

"Huh. So how did you get to that?"

"Well, the thing is, Beatrice, from my work as an artist. It tries to deal with politics, history, humour, even religion occasionally. These are some of my ingredients. So I just applied that approach to the teaching jobs I looked for."

"Thank you. I hoped you would say that. The Pratt Institute has many academic departments as well as Art & Design. We would like to see some interfacing."

"Yes, I read that aspiration from the description of the position here. It interested me."

Beatrice turns to the Chair. "May I ask Vaughan just one more thing? I think it is important."

"Sure, Beatrice. Shoot."

"Vaughan, your resumé says you are now married to a New Yorker, who lives in the city, but you have a young daughter in England. If we hire you, would this work out for you and, equally importantly, for them?"

"Er . . . yes, I would hope so."

"You would *hope* so? You would not be conflicted . . . your head would not be in two places at once?"

Where is this woman going? I must be looking puzzled. Will they see I'm now sweating?

"Let me put it this way, Vaughan. And correct me if I am out of line, out of tune . . . you know. It seems to me that your work and can-do way is very American. I like that. But are you yourself emotionally rooted in England?"

"I don't understand." (I do understand.)

"Okay. In a nutshell. Your art in America, your heart in England?"

Beatrice is smart. Too smart.

"Oh. Why do you say that?"

"Maybe because I am a psychotherapist. Amongst other things. Maybe that."

The Chair intervenes. "Beatrice. Just maybe we are getting a little too personal?"

He now puts his own spin on it.

"You see, Vaughan, working here at Pratt, we don't see just as a job. We see ourselves as a family. Which you may join."

He's thrown me a lifeline. But my brain is racing. Of course. That meeting with the Dean of the Faculty at Massachusetts when I handed him my resignation letter. We had agreed any reference should say I resigned to return to the UK so I could see my young daughter regularly following my divorce. But I've since married a New Yorker – on the rebound, for sure. So why have they invited me, a flaky, confused candidate, as one of only two finalists for the key job of running their art school? Unless . . . they didn't have that reference when they selected the two finalists. That has to be it. You'll have to answer. Look at them looking at you. Intensely.

"Well, I would very much like to join you at the Pratt Institute. A distinguished school. But please, rest assured I can work those personal matters out."

"Okay. I'm sure you can, Vaughan. Are there any more questions for Vaughan? I know you were both at Vaughan's presentation last week and you discussed a bunch of stuff then."

The Chair is looking in the direction of the heads of Graphic Design and Visual Arts. They smile but shake their heads. They may not be voting for me.

"Well, Vaughan. If you have any questions yourself, you can take those up with the President, Ted here, who will now be taking you for lunch. So all we have to do is thank you so much for attending and criss-crossing the Atlantic! We really appreciate that."

The River Café, Water Street, Brooklyn, New York.

"You like seafood, Vaughan? They do a good seafood platter down here."

The driver pulls the President's Mercedes into the restaurant parking lot right by the Brooklyn Bridge.

"I do, Ted."

"Great, Vaughan. Let's eat and talk."

Outside the car now and the thunder of traffic on the bridge deck above makes further conversation impossible. It's not far to the restaurant door. How do I play this? Am I in too deep?

"Enjoy the chardonnay, Vaughan. No, I won't. I'll take a Perrier water." Ted waves the waiter away.

"So, Vaughan. I trust you were satisfied with our interview process."

"Very much so, Ted."

"Is there any one thing you liked, you appreciated?"

"Oh, yes. Being deeply interested in my work as an artist. I'm afraid, at this level of appointment, that is something often ignored in the UK. Nowadays anyway."

"Really? Why so?"

"A cult of managerialism brought in under Mrs Thatcher. A new breed of business managers seems to have emerged in England. They can be hired to run anything. It happened when I was here in America."

"Well, we hear good things about Margaret Thatcher over here. The other side of the coin, I guess. Anyway, you had some business experience yourself in Nottingham."

"That is true. But it wasn't until ten years later that part of my history became of interest, indeed fashionable, in English higher education."

"I see, Vaughan. Now, talking of business, would you mind if I go to, I guess, the bottom line?"

I put down my glass.

"Vaughan, what sort of remuneration would you be looking for? Just give me a straight-up figure."

This is it. Do you want to be here or not? I give him a figure. An outrageous one.

Ted leans back, his face impassive.

"Okaaaaay. So. Let's take a peek at those menus. As I said, their fish is good."

We're on a road to nowhere
Come on inside
Takin' that ride to nowhere
We'll take that ride

I'm in a small helicopter flying from Manhattan to Kennedy. Part of the Concorde package. Top of my game and just been interviewed for the headship of the best art school in America. The view of Manhattan is quite amazing. And I've never felt more miserable or more alone, my only companion that David Byrne song now firmly stuck in my head.

Understandably and deservedly, the other candidate got the job.

KENT INSTITUTE OF ART & DESIGN, 1996

I didn't apply for another job for six years. But plenty happened in my life during that time, much of it good. I ran the art school at Walsall, carried on making my own art, although I did not have the time to promote it or exhibit it very much because of the pressure of the job. Most importantly, in 1991 I met Polly and we have been together since. We have two grown-up offspring. But in 1995, a terrible thing happened. Our elder child, Hattie, then two and a half, was diagnosed with leukaemia. She was placed under the care of London's famous Great Ormond Street Hospital for Children. So when the opportunity arose for a job in the south-east, I applied. It was the Directorship of the Kent Institute of Art & Design, or KIAD, a university-level institution comprising the long-established and well-respected art colleges of Canterbury, Maidstone and Rochester. KIAD had two and a half thousand art, design and architecture students.

Bridgewood Manor Hotel, just off the M2, Kent.

"Professor Grylls?"

"That's me."

"Yes, here you are. Room 206. Here is your key. Did you come by car?"

"Oh, thanks. Yes, it's in the car park."

"You'll need this pass. Just place it on the dashboard. While you're doing that I can arrange for this to be taken up to your room."

She gestures towards my small suitcase.

"No worries. I'll take it. And then I"ll find my room."

"Of course. As you like. By the way, your party – Kent Institute of Art & Design isn't it ? – will be meeting in the lounge off the bar in the half hour before dinner. That's at seven p.m. in the Charles Dickens Suite, which is just through there. You can't miss it. Some of them are in the bar already."

I nod, walk out to the car park, deposit the parking pass and head back into the hotel as discreetly as possible. I don't want to see all those people until the last possible moment. I'm bound to know some of the candidates. I'll keep my head down, head for my room. Avoid the lift and take the stairs.

Now in my room. Unpack. Hang up suit. Lay out overheads on table. Take out exhibition catalogues. I'll only take one into the final interview. Will decide which one tomorrow. This is going to be a long haul. Dinner tonight. Presentation tomorrow. Final interview at the college the day after. And here I am stuck in an hotel by a motorway with nothing else in sight apart from the other candidates. And, most troubling by far, our daughter Hattie yet again back in hospital. Must keep that quiet. They won't want a director with personal stress to deal with. Oh no.

"So, ladies and gentleman, just to brief you before the first course arrives. You all have name tags. And you all have a list. So, each candidate for the directorship has a governor sitting on either side of them. So, during each course, can governors chat to the candidate on their right for the first part of their course. and to their left for the second part. Then all governors will change places. The same will happen for the second and third course and then for coffee. So please, governors, please consult your list which tells you which governor will be changing places with which governor and when. And to remind everyone when it is time to turn your conversation to the other candidate or governor, I shall be ringing this bell."

The Chairman produces a small bell. He demonstrates it vigorously.

I glance at my list and turn to my left.

"Hello. I'm Vaughan Grylls. And you are Colonel FitzAlan."

The rest – a blur of musical chairs with me not feeling too well and having our daughter Hattie in the back of my mind. I'll ring Polly from my room as soon as this charade is over.

"Well, what would you feel about the present Director joining the Board of Governors, should you be appointed?"

I look Governor Joyce in the eye. This is an absurd suggestion. Does she really mean it? I think she does. She is scanning my face quite anxiously for a reply.

"It would be highly unusual in a university-level institution."

Saved by the bell from further discussion and none other than Dr Henry Kirk, Chair of Governors, saviour in hand, heads in my direction.

"I could come home tonight and drive back here tomorrow. My presentation isn't until midday."

"No, Hattie is okay. Another bout of measles."

"All caused by knocking out the immune system to deal with the leukaemia. People think it's the leukaemia but it isn't. Are you sure I should stay?"

"Absolutely. Especially as you sound as though you're coming down with a cold. You don't want to give her something else. Anything else tonight?"

"Well, the Chair wants us to meet senior staff informally over a drink at the bar so I might stick my head round the door. Not that I want to."

"Oh, I think you should. Just do it briefly. Then go to bed."

Oh dear. One of the candidates is Gerald Monger, that ghastly fellow I inherited at Walsall. I got rid of him by giving a humdinger of a reference. Felt bad about that but was desperate. Now, let's see. I'll move to the other end of the bar where those two older guys are standing. I'll ask them if they are candidates, governors or staff. Neither is wearing a badge. But neither am I. I've taken mine off. I hate them.

"Hello. I'm Vaughan Grylls, one of the candidates."

"Yes, we know. Hello, Vaughan. I'm Paul. Paul Laslett. Remember me?"

Of course. How embarrassing. He was head of photography at that Surrey art school when I did some visiting teaching down there. And he gave me that reference for America. I was thankful for that as I didn't want to ask the terrible Kevin Crumb.

"I'm sorry, Paul. I didn't recognise you across a crowded room. But I do now! What are you doing here?"

"I'm an Assistant Director at the Kent Institute of Art & Design. Bit longer in the tooth I'm afraid. Hair gone. That is probably why you didn't recognise me. By the way, this is Rodney. Rodney Hipkiss. He is also an Assistant Director."

"Pleased to meet you, Rodney. So how many Assistant Directors are there?"

"Three. I'm in charge of marketing and head of Maidstone College, Rodney is finance and head of Canterbury College, and Pete Griffin, who isn't here, is academic and head of Rochester College."

"Oh, great. So do you think that the shortlist of seven candidates is good, Paul?"

"Well, yes, Vaughan. Although I felt I should have been on it."

"So should I," interjects Rodney, glumly.

"Oh?"

"We were told, Vaughan. That we weren't being shortlisted. But it was the way we were told."

I ignore this and press forward to what I want to know.

"So, will you both be interviewing the candidates?"

"Not formally," says Paul.

"They'll ask us, just for form's sake, but they won't take any notice," says Rodney.

"They won't even do that, Rodney. It was worse for me. At least I had attended art school."

I turn to Rodney. "What is your background, Rodney?"

"Accountancy. I'm an accountant."

"I see. So what do you think they should be looking for in a new Director?"

"Someone who thinks about the cost of new courses before starting them."

"Okay. What about you, Paul?"

"Someone with vision for new courses. And who will support our overseas student recruitment. We have over three hundred now. All paying full fees."

"Keeps the wolf from the door," says Rodney. "Paul is responsible for the overseas student success. I''ll give him that."

"I could have done more. But one of the Governors stuck his head round my office door one day – didn't even knock – and said, "We're not shortlisting you." So I asked why and he said, "You are too old." Just like that. Then he was gone. Didn't even come into my office It was hurtful."

Paul studies me mournfully for a reaction. Is he about to burst into tears? But no time. Rodney caps him.

"It was worse for me than for Paul. A Governor stuck his head around my door, just the same, didn't even knock, and said, "We're not shortlisting you." So I asked why and he said, "When's the last time you went to the Tate Gallery?" so I said I've never been to the Tate Gallery and he said, "And that is why we don't want you as Director." Then he was gone. Didn't even come into my office. Not nice."

"Well, you are both agreed on the importance of overseas students' income. We have built it up in my present job but not to that extent."

I decide to move away as this conversation is exhausted and, anyway, over Rodney's shoulder I can see Gerald Monger heading in my direction. I do not want to engage in banter there.

"I am very sorry to hear about how you were both treated. But I must go. I need an early night. Well, it was very nice talking to you, Paul, and you, Rodney."

"Vaughan. Good luck tomorrow. And the day after. You'd make a good Director."

"Thank you, Paul. Much appreciated."

There must be thirty of them eyeing me up in the Great Expectations Conference Suite at the Bridgewood Manor Hotel as I enter clutching my transparencies for their overhead projector – which I am praying will work – for the twenty minutes I have been allotted to wax forth on the topic given to me: "Kent Institute of Art & Design – the next five to ten years". What can one say? I couldn't talk on "Vaughan Grylls – the next five to ten years".

But needs must. So on and on I wax, not flitting about but standing fixed to the spot as Polly advised when I went through my rehearsal with her as my audience of one two days ago. So now I've reached the end, thank God, standing still and with no obvious balls-ups. I don't think so anyway.

It is now the following day and I am out of that hotel and at the college, sitting outside the Board Room. A woman candidate from Sunderland is in there now. Opposite me is a candidate from Loughborough and next to him the ghastly Gerald Monger.

About an hour ago, the Kent Institute Secretary to the Governors, who could be a funeral director, came up to me with a piece of paper and asked me to ring the number he had scribbled down on it. The fellow from Loughborough kindly offered me his mobile phone so I could do it straight-away. I went out into the corridor and rang, and it was University College Hospital. My hands were shaking with fear. But it was fine as it was just a message to say that Hattie was to be discharged at six p.m. and could she be picked up? Then I remember I had given the Institute's phone number in case of emergency. I must keep all this quiet.

It was the same funeral director chap who told me after my presen-tation yesterday, as he was helping me pack up my overheads, that the ex-ternal assessor for this job, who will be in that interview room right now, is an artist and is the head of a well-known art school. So the chances are they are looking for an artist to run their art school which is unique amongst all the interviews I've had in this country since returning from America.

The woman candidate has now come out and the man who lent me his phone has gone in. That leaves me and Monger.

"Are you showing them your art works, Gerald?"

"No, of course not, Vaughan. This is an administrative leadership role."

"Of course."

Silence. We both gaze out of the large, modernist windows.

"Gerald. Do you have a catalogue of your work with you?"

"No. Of course not. As I said, this is an administrative leadership role."

Silence. More gazing out of the windows.

The door opens. The man who lent me his phone emerges followed by the Institute Secretary who raises his eyebrows in my direction.

"Professor Grylls. You are on next. Could you give us a couple of minutes? To allow for comfort breaks. I'll be right back."

I nod. Two men exit for their comfort breaks and are joined by the Institute Secretary for his.

I look over to Monger. The moment has arrived.

"Well. Good luck, Vaughan."

The Institute Secretary has returned. He looks in my direction.

"After you, Professor Grylls."

I stand up, take the large catalogue of my American and South African exhibition with its colour covers out of my case, making sure Gerald Monger sees it, and head for the door.

"Thanks, Gerald. Good luck to you."

Hattie recovered, although she did have one more relapse, a few months later. I was Director of the Kent Institute of Art & Design for nine years, the second longest I have spent anywhere. It was, just as my predecessor said it would be, a wonderful job. I had a terrific team and I made sure I continued teaching whenever I could. Although I didn't have time to promote my own work, I did continue making it.

My Chairman of Governors was terrific but I made two miscalculations in the last two years that would prove fatal both for my academic career and the Kent Institute of Art & Design. The first was a disastrous appointment I made to the headship of a major academic department. The second, and even more disastrous, which I instigated on the poor advice of a government auditor, was persuading my long-standing and totally dedicated Chair of Governors to retire. His successor was, well . . .

LONDON INSTITUTE OF LAW, 2005

In 2003 the government allowed the establishment of specialist universities, provided they had at least 6,000 students. So I thought: why not merge the Kent Institute of Art & Design with the Surrey Institute of Art & Design to form a new creative arts university with 6,500 students? At least it would get the Universty of Kent off our backs, for they were always trying to take us over. At best we would have more clout in teaching and research and less back-office cost. And I planned to retire in 2007 and get back full-time to my own studio, so I had a personal motive. But the previous year I had taken the advice of a government auditor who had opined that my wonderful chair of governors had been in office too long and I should therefore bring in a successor. Which I did. Gavin Drane.

"And then on Thursday, Vaughan, you have a meeting at the Law Institute."

"Really, Anna?"

"Yes. Celia, the project manager, put it in your diary. It was there when I got back from lunch."

"Huh? Odd."

"What is this meeting about, Celia? I don't think you should have put it in my diary without discussing it first with me or Anna, my PA."

"Oh, neither of you was around. It is just an opportunity for you to chat about the future of the new university with Gavin Drane and Gordon Black. In an interview situation."

"An interview situation?"

"Gavin, about this interview situation. What is it? Who is going to be there?"

"Oh, Vaughan. I'm surprised you have not been more fully briefed by Celia. Just an opportunity for you and Doreen, your opposite number at Surrey, to share views with myself and Gordon on how the Executive will operate in our new University for the Creative Arts."

"But we've done all that – me as Chief Executive for two years until I retire, looking after the back office and the money, and Doreen as Rector looking after all things academic."

"Yes. Of course. Interview is probably too strong a word . . ."

I'm stepping out of the lift at the law institute where Gavin works, and I see – no it can't be, yes it is, the project manager, Celia, hurrying out of Gavin's office like the White Rabbit. She sees me, stops in her tracks and heads in the opposite direction. I walk down the corridor and knock on the half-open door.

"Come in." But that is not Gavin's voice.

But Gavin is inside. He is sitting on his desk, legs dangling. Gordon, Chair of Governors at Surrey, the one who invited me into the office, is seated in a chair. Gordon gets up, shakes hands and waves me to the other chair. Gavin continues dangling his legs.

"Has Doreen arrived?"

"No, we are seeing her separately."

"Oh, I thought we were all meeting together, Gordon."

"There's been a change of plan. Sorry."

A pause.

"What would be your personal view on the qualities or otherwise of Martin?"

Eh? Martin, Doreen's deputy?

"Well, he is still young . . . could be a future CEO. So for succession planning we should do all we can to keep him on board."

Gordon and Gavin nod to one another like those toy dogs you see in the backs of cars.

"So what about the other members of the Executive?"

"Well, I am supportive of each of them, Gordon. A good team for the future of a new university."

Another pause. Gordon looks at Gavin who still hasn't said a word. He turns back to me.

"We've received written reports from Celia, the project manager, on each of these senior staff."

"Oh? But Celia reports to myself and Doreen and I haven't asked her to do them. Neither has Doreen, as far as I know."

"The governing bodies of both institutions commissioned the reports."

"Really? It hasn't been mentioned at any Governors' meetings."

"Well, they have, Vaughan. Would you like to hear them?"

"Well, I can read them after this meeting."

"No, we would like to read them out to you now."

"Okay, Gordon, if it is that urgent."

Gavin looks down at his dangling feet. Gordon leans across in front of Gavin and picks up a sheaf of papers from Gavin's desk. He starts reading out short, bland and utterly forgettable comments.

"Well, Vaughan. Would you agree that these reports support your views on these senior staff?"

"Yes, but they don't really shed any more light on what we know already."

"Would you further agree that Celia has been objective?"

I nod, but I cannot see the point of such a fruitless exercise.

Another pause.

"We now come to the report on you."

He turns to Gavin who eases himself down from his desk-top. He has been sitting on something. Another report. The one on me? It is. His hands shake as he picks it up. It must be warm from his bottom. He starts to read it out. It is longer than all the others put together. And it is not bland. In fact it is a crudely cobbled-together piece of petty charges. In any other circumstance it would have been laughable to hear.

"Gavin. What does it mean when Celia writes that I appear bored when certain people speak in meetings?"

"What she says, Vaughan. But let's move on."

"I appear tired when certain people speak in meetings?"

"Yes. That is what she has written. But she is objective. As you admit. So let's move on."

"'He did not stay at an hotel the night before an away-day and thus forewent a supper with the project manager and the senior executive.'"

"But Gavin, that is ridiculous and unfair. In fact, it is completely inappropriate. My mother had just died. Celia knew that. I rang her immediately. And you also knew as I rang you, too."

"All right, Vaughan. I won't read any more out from this report on you as there is enough here."

"Enough for what? You will of course give me a copy so I can thoroughly refute Celia's charges?"

Gordon steps in.

"I'm afraid we cannot, Vaughan."

"Why?"

"Because it is confidential."

"But this is . . . Orwellian, Gavin!"

Gordon's monkey hoists his arse back on the desk. He contemplates his dangling feet again. He prefers them to looking me in the eye. Gordon leans forward menacingly.

"The governors of both institutions have commissioned these, as we have said."

Then, at last, the penny drops in my slow brain. These so-called reports are a crude device to dress up this meeting as objective and fair. This is simply an attempt to get rid of me so as to guarantee Surrey a takeover rather than a merger.

Gavin has been thinking about my last comment. He has to cover himself in front of Gordon. Now he looks up from those feet of his.

"I was surprised and shocked to receive this report on you, Vaughan. I had no idea it was going to be as bad as this."

"Gavin, Celia's trumped-up and patently thin allegations are more surprising and shocking for me to hear than for you!"

"Maybe, but I do have to say, Vaughan, that what she has written here gives voice to that which I have felt for some time. In fact, there were more allegations of my own I could add."

"But you can't have it both ways, Gavin, be surprised and not surprised. Anyway, what allegations of your own do you have?"

"Okay. You spent too much money on lawyers' fees in the legal dispute with the University of Kent."

"No, you did, Gavin – you sent at least twenty emails in two weeks telling our lawyers to take out two separate actions. That put up the bills. I'll show those emails to Gordon if you want. I've got the trail."

Gavin slides his gaze nervously towards his new master. The new master is beginning to look very impatient. So I say:

"Gavin, why have you have raked up an internal Kent Institute matter? We are now establishing the University for the Creative Arts from a merger of equals. That is far preferable to all that old stuff with the University of Kent."

Gavin nods and looks back down at the feet. He has given up. But Gordon hasn't. He needs to get in an allegation of his own. And it is the one that made him decide to sack me.

"Vaughan. Do you remember the meeting on the financial regulations for the new university?"

"Of course, Gordon. It was at my house in Islington. Only a couple of weeks ago. You were there, as was I."

"You altered the minutes."

"No, the finance director took the minutes and in emailing round his draft omitted two items we had agreed. So he re-circulated with those points in. In any case, they are unconfirmed minutes to be agreed at the next meeting in a few days. When the institution is a legal entity."

Gordon brushes me aside.

"You added these points because as the future chief executive you wanted to make sure that staffing establishment control remained with you and the finance director reports to you. I cannot recall agreeing that."

"Well, that is what we all agreed. And you were there, Gordon. Drinking my tea and eating my biscuits."

I see a flash of hatred in his eyes. Then it is gone.

"Vaughan, do you not trust Doreen and her academic heads to spend their budgets accordingly?"

"Of course. But there has to be a final place of control on the principal expenditure line in the institution or we could end up with, should our finance director's estimate be correct, a £2 million deficit if spending patterns, particularly at the Surrey end, continue at the same level."

Gordon stares at me and I stare back. Will he back down? Will he hell.

I look at Gavin, who shrugs. Gavin Drane is my boss. Gordon Black is not my boss. Not for a few days, anyway. But the problem is my boss has thrown in the towel before this meeting – sorry, interview.

"Vaughan. I have to say that it is my job, as chair-designate, to sum up today's interview."

"Okay, Gordon."

"Celia's advice to us is that you will be a risk to the future of the new institution. Therefore you must accept severance. You should take garden leave immediately and not return to your office. You can now go and consider the offer we will be making shortly. This interview is now over."

I get up. I do not shake hands but stagger out. Gavin follows. We then stand next to one another in the lift without exchanging glances.

Now outside. At least the sun is warm.

"We'll be as generous as we can be as long as you leave without a fuss. We can issue an agreed statement. I"ll do my very best to get you an honour in view of the fact that you actually invented this merger – and you've done a hell of a lot nationally. Er . . . we may even be able to name a building after you."

"All that doesn't mean anything to me. That was a kangaroo court, Gavin. A kangaroo court!"

"We have to get on with them. We were trying to hear all sides."

"Nothing to do with sides, Gavin. Gordon wants me out of the way because Surrey do not want my hand on the money tap. They want a takeover! And now they've got it! Thanks to you, Gavin!"

Looking down at his shoes yet again, he turns on his heel and walks back into the building. That wasn't quite fair. All he did was roll over. And it was me who persuaded him to become my Chair of Governors in the first place. You stupid ass, Vaughan. I turn in the direction of home. I'll walk back. It may make me feel less nauseous.

As I suspected, the document had not been commissioned by the Governors. But that point was overtaken, for a couple of weeks later I received an entirely different one from Surrey's lawyers who obviously saw Celia's attempt as amateurish and flimsy. Theirs was much shorter, asserting that I and Doreen did not get on. Therefore one of us must go. And that, of course, meant me.

TIME OUT IN A HACKNEY STUDIO, 2009

In 2006 I was in my first show in London since 1988. It was held at the Fieldgate Gallery in Whitechapel. At the Private View I overhead one visitor saying to another, "Vaughan Grylls. Now there's a name from the past! He must still be alive then?" Although I had continued making my work throughout many years in academe, that remark was in a way flattering, because to most young curators and art critics I was unheard of. Their world and that of running art universities does not overlap. So although I did not expect to get back my former notoriety, nor would I want or need to, some recognition is always nice, even if it consists of someone's surprise that one is still alive and kicking.

My breakthrough, if that is not too grand a description, came when I was offered a show at Sadler's Wells Theatre. The foyer exhibition area was ideal and I showed ten life-sized photographic portraits of actors playing fearless women my mother had admired such as Vera Brittain, Marie Stopes and Mary Wollstonecraft. I saw my exhibition as a tribute to my mother who had died in the middle of my merger – sorry, takeover – battles. That it was shown at Sadler's Wells acknowledged her past as she was a hoofer in musicals when she first met my father. It was a Pygmalion marriage of people from different sides of the tracks.

In early 2009, Helen Sumpter from Time Out *came to view my new works and interview me before* Mother *was sent for exhibition at Sadler's Wells.*

"So, Vaughan, are you celebrating your mother or the women she admired?"

"Both, Helen. She left school at twelve, you know. A war widow's daughter. To earn money she became a dancer on the stage. She started in the Theatre Royal in Nottingham selling programmes."

"What about your dad?"

"Well, he had been to Oxford. He was a teacher and seventeen years older than her. They married when she had just turned eighteen."

"What did his family think?"

"Not much. Well, they shunned the wedding, although one of his brothers turned up. When my father died, a sister of his rang me up and said he should never have married a 'common showgirl'. I told her to fuck off and hung up."

"Oh. So how did she get to know about these women?"

"Through my father. He introduced her to a middle-class world of ideas, although some of it she found puzzling such as overhearing a conversation between him and his headmaster about whether a new teacher was enjoying his job. She had never thought of an employer worrying about an employee enjoying their job or not. Even dancing on the stage. You were paid to do it and you did it. Whether you liked your job or not was irrelevant."

"She sounds an interesting person."

"Yes, strong personality. Striking looking. Liberal outlook. Against war and cruelty. Thought sex pretty harmless. She was in the Peace Pledge Union during the war. As a child I remember her in tears at the kitchen table the morning Ruth Ellis was hanged. She had been up to London a few days before to hand in a letter to the Home Secretary. Ellis is one of the people in the show."

"Yes. It is a particularly strong one, I think."

"Ruth Ellis took the blame for one of her two lovers, you know. He handed her the gun and drove her to a pub where the other lover was drinking. But she kept that quiet. He got off scot-free. Not even an accessory to murder. But there was such an outcry, and so Ruth Ellis was the last woman to be hanged in Britain."

"Wasn't she played by Miranda Richardson in a film?"

"She was. She also inspired a previous film with Diana Dors playing the part. It was called *Yield to the Night*. I remember it. You're probably too young to remember it, though."

"Yes. Quite. But why have you made these portraits life-size?"

"Well, it was partly the relationship to the type of full-length dressing mirror which my mother used to check herself in before going out. She was always well turned out. But also I've been recently to see the Isenheim altarpiece by Matthias Grunewald and I also wanted something of the uncompromising directness of his crucifixion images."

"So what other artists do you admire? Who would be among your top ten inspirational figures?"

"Probably, in this country at least, Richard Hamilton, Eduardo Paolozzi and John Latham. They are uncompromising."

"Well, thank you for showing me these. But just one thing more – how do you like being a full-time artist again?"

"Well . . . obviously the art world now is very different from when I was first making and showing work in the 1970s. In some ways I feel like I'm an emerging artist all over again. But I'm no YBA. I'm an EVOBA – an Emerging Very Old British artist."

SUNDAY SUPPLEMENT VISITS KENT, 2012

In the early summer of 2012 I had an exhibition in a West End gallery. The gallery's PR agency arranged for me to be interviewed at our east Kent house for a Sunday newspaper colour supplement just before the show opened. The newspaper had a series running about odd houses and odd owners, so I was now invited to join.

A taxi pulls through the gate and out jumps a petite young woman in jeans and a tee shirt. She scans the house in front of her and then sees me.

"Hi! Are you Vaughan?"

"Yes, I am. Welcome."

"Thank you. Hi. I'm Anna."

I walk up to the taxi by which time its driver has opened the boot and taken out a wheely case with a tripod strapped to it.

"Pleased to meet you, Anna."

"We found you at last. This house looks . . . beautiful. A long way from anywhere . . ."

"You can say that again." The taxi driver, back in the driver's seat and clearly waiting to be paid, has spoken.

Anna darts up with the money. "Can you pick me up in three hours?"

"That's okay, Anna. I"ll drive you back to the station."

"You sure?"

"Of course."

The driver shrugs, starts his engine and turns the car out of the drive.

Anna speaks excellent English but she is clearly not English.

"Where are you from, Anna?"

"I'm Spanish. Actually, I'm a Catalan, Vaughan. There is a difference."

I nod. "Of course. But are you photographing and interviewing as well? My gallery said two people were coming."

"Yes. I'm just the photographer. Holly should be here. But something came up. She wants to say sorry. Sorry. Sorry. I love that English word. Holly will call you. Tomorrow okay? When I have shown her the photographs."

"Holly sorry?"

Anna throws back her head and laughs.

"You are humour sense."

Into the house we go and for the next three hours, Anna photographs everything in sight while I move furniture as requested while attempting more cracks about the English language.

"So, Vaughan. Sorry about yesterday. I would have loved to be there. Especially after seeing these great pics."

"Yes. I thought Anna did a good job. She works like a dynamo."

"She does, Vaughan. Now. The interview bit. I'm going to put you on speakerphone. I'll type my copy straight in. Is that okay?"

"Fine. Carry on."

"Great. So . . . why do you work out in the country?"

"Well, I make my work in London as well. Like the life-sized aeroplane I made last year out of old family photographs. The engines I made in London, the fuselage and wings down here."

"Oh, yeah. I checked that one out. The autobiographical one. You showed it in Dalston. Great work."

"Well, in the sense of big. A nineteen-metre wingspan of a Second World War Dornier bomber. It was autobiographical because it was a facsimile of the type of plane that shot at me while I was a baby in a pram. But my grandmother pulled the pram out of the way just in time. Which is why I called the work *Grandmother*. As a tribute to her. The people and events in the old photos I made the plane from just wouldn't have existed had she been slower."

"Great. Terrific. But being down at that house in Kent. What is it like?

"The house or me?"

"Both!"

"Well, the thing is, being an artist, it's useless if you have lots of people around you, you never get anything done. You have to get away. No one talks to you about contemporary art down here – no one cares. You're incognito as an artist. So I can get on with things."

I can hear Holly tapping away in the background. I pause to let her catch up.

"And . . ."

"You want me to go on?"

"Yeah. Let's talk about that lovely house."

"Well, it was supposedly built in 1386 but the brick exterior is dated 1702. But I like the setting equally. Orchards. Farming country. Very un-home counties. A bit rough at the edges. And less than two hours from London. And near the Channel Tunnel. It suits us and it reminds me of the flat, windswept landscape of my childhood. Large skies . . . you know."

"Great. Those logs in that big fireplace."

"Oh, they are the remains of Leylandii trees we chopped down. Enough wood to burn for years. If you put one of those logs on the fire on Christmas Eve it'll still be burning on New Year's Day."

"Great! Okay. That old car on the drive? Looks brilliant."

Tap, tap, tap. Tap tap tap.

"It is a Bristol car I've owned for years. It's an eccentric British classic nobody has ever heard of – a bit like me."

"Okay! But I've heard of you, And, you know what? I'd just love to go in that car. You took Anna back to the station in it yesterday. She told me."

"Oh did she? She thought it was fun?"

"She did, Vaughan. She did. So, just to carry on here, you went to Goldsmiths and the Slade and you made pun sculptures in the 1960s. And in some pics Anna has done in your studio, you are holding *A Case for Wittgenstein* made in, er . . ."

"1969."

"Wow. A long time ago. Let's see. Fifteen years before I was born.

And that pun sculpture will be in your show at the Piper Gallery."

"Yes."

"Why, er, Wittgenstein?"

"He was a linguistic philosopher. Didn't understand much of what he said but his picture theory of language made some sense to me . You know, 'Statements are only meaningful if they can be pictured in the real world.' That is what he said."

"Okay. Can you repeat that, Vaughan? So I can get it down correctly."

"Yes, of course, Holly. Wittgenstein said, 'Statements are only meaningful if they can be pictured in the real world.' You and me . . . well, aren't we trying to do that now?"

"Right! Okay. I'm looking at the living room. And that sculpture under the grand piano. The black-and-white round one."

"*The Drunken Clergyman.* Even older. 1967."

"Tell me about him."

"Well, he is a cross between a dog-collared vicar and an Irish coffee. I got the idea from my first-ever Irish coffee. I drank lots of them in a Berni Inn in Tamworth, Staffordshire, and then I went into a churchyard opposite to sleep them off and I was woken by a vicar so I had this dog-collar looking down at me and saying, 'Come on, mate. Up you get.' So I then filled it with a liquid so when you push him, he makes a slurping sound."

"I just love him. Will he be in the show?"

"He will indeed. He is the oldest work I have and certainly the oldest in the show. He is the only one I kept from my time as a student at Walsall and he has moved with me ever since. The last thing I did before I left my last home was put him in the front seat and drive off."

"In your old car? Right. Now what about those photo-montages? Your gallery says your first was a photo-mosaic dated 1978 which was chosen for the Whitechapel Gallery by its then director, a young Nicholas Serota."

"Yes. A 360-degree view of the interior of Hagia Sophia, Istanbul. I made it as a photo-mosaic to mirror the subject. And then I did the same sort of thing the following year photographing the Wailing Wall, Jerusalem – you know, building up the photo-montage in the same way the wall itself was built."

"Okay. Any others?"

"Lots."

"Can I have just one more before we go to your upcoming show?"

"Okay. My *Site of the Assassination of President Kennedy.* The photo-montage followed the lines of fire. Except I was using a a telephoto camera instead of a gun."

"How big was that?"

"About nine metres wide. Two and a half metres high."

"Okay. Now about the new work for this show. Tell me about one of them. Is that large cross of black-and-white photos in your studio one of them?"

"Yes. It's made of photographs taken in St Petersburg, in this church where the last tsar's remains lie. Standing there was a woman who was explaining, in graphic detail, what had happened to the tsar and his family to a deaf and dumb tour group. She was explaining it in sign language. So I put a video camera on her, freeze-framed the best images and put them together in the form of the Russian cross."

"And what is that work called?"

"Signs of the Cross."

"Silly me. It would be. The Grylls taste for puns shows no sign of weakening, then?"

"Certainly not, Holly. Certainly not."

The colour supplement article appeared one Sunday a few weeks later. It felt strange looking at pictures in a newspaper of our house while actually sitting in the house.

ENFIELD UNIVERSITY, 2013

Although I had got back into the swing of being a full-time artist, I was getting lonely working in my studio all day and I particularly missed engagement with students, so when I saw an advertisement for a job I fancied, I applied. Although I was shortlisted, I was never interviewed. The correspondence says all you need to know.

Dear Vice-Chancellor,

I thought I should write to you about an interview process I experienced at Enfield University recently.

Following a short email exchange with Professor Heather Wrightson who, as part of the advertisement for the post of Professor in Contemporary World Practices in Art, had invited contact, I applied, explaining as advised by Heather that I was interested in it on a part-time basis.

On 18 March I received an email from Des Veitch, School of Art & Design Executive Officer, inviting me for interview for the post of Professor in Design on the following Thursday, 28 March, the day before Good Friday. She then sent a correction saying I was being called for interview not for Reader in Design (sic), but for Professor in Contemporary World Practices in Art or Design.

As I had arranged to fly to Italy on 28 March for Easter, I replied immediately saying I would be back in the UK directly after the Easter holiday on 2 April. I asked whether there was a more suitable day for the interview.

Des then suggested a Skype interview on 28 March and I replied that we could try, although in my experience Skype to and from Italy was erratic. (My daughter is at university in Venice so I know!) Nevertheless, I could definitely be in phone contact that day. Des Veitch said she would try and swap me for another candidate so we could at least try the Skype interview at 4.30 p.m. UK time. I agreed, although with some misgivings.

Two days then passed so I emailed Des with my Skype ID asking whether Enfield wanted to call me or me them. If the latter could I have their ID?

On 21 March Des replied saying Enfield would Skype me on the ID I had given on 28 March at 4.30 p.m. UK time.

As I was concerned about using Skype, a concern increased by the fact that I was the one who had instigated offering my Skype ID, I emailed Professor Heather Wrightson on 21 March:

I understand from Des that you can only interview next Thursday when unfortunately I shall be in Italy, returning p.m Tuesday 2 April.

I am happy for a Skype as proposed – notwithstanding Italian telecoms not always being great – but I did wonder whether the Skype proposal should be supplemented by an informal meeting between us, given the importance of the post. I can find time Tuesday or Wednesday next week or on my return.

I would like to hear your views on creating more than the sum of the parts from your new research environment, informed by the individual research of your recently appointed professoriate – which looks great, by the way – to which I would contribute, should I work for you. That, and of course the REF submission . . .

I look forward to hearing from you.

On 22 March Heather replied:

I have asked the Deputy VC, Hassan Ansari, about this as he is chairing the interview panels. Being in Italy is a problem worth having! Enjoy it.

The Skype interview did not work. So on the day it should have taken place I emailed Heather:

I'm sorry we weren't able to talk today. I was really looking forward to it. Italian technology clearly got the better of us! Do let me know if there is another opportunity to talk as I would value it.

Have a good Easter.

On 18 April, having not received a reply, I emailed Heather Wrightson again:

I don't know whether you received my email of the evening of 28 March as you may have been away for the holidays.

For the interview that day my Skype address did not receive a request from Enfield. So from Italy, approximately fifteen minutes after the scheduled interview time, I called Des who said she could not get in touch with you as you were in another building. When I had finished speaking with Des, I picked up your message saying you were trying to Skype without success. I was probably on the phone to Des when you called. I tried to call you back but as ring-back wasn't accepted on the number you had called from, I couldn't do so. I called Des back and asked her for your Skype address. She found it, I tried it but couldn't get through that way. So I called Des a third time. Someone else answered who said she had left for the day.

I had arranged a fast connection through a professional communications company in Tuscany which has proved pretty reliable – certainly for Italy – in the past. It may be that our respective Skype upgrades may not have been compatible. It could have been any number of things.

I was looking forward to discussing a strategy proposal I had prepared for interview when I could also have discussed my working for you on a part-time basis. However, I'm not clear where the interview process is right now.

As I have not received a reply to this email either, I am wondering whether Enfield University is experiencing electronic communication problems. That would also help explain why the University had difficulty in contacting me via Skype on 28 March. So, just to be sure, I am writing to you by the traditional method.

I do hope I hear from you.

Yours sincerely,

Vaughan Grylls

Dear Professor Grylls,

I refer to your letter of the 28th April 2013 received into the Vice-Chancellor's office this morning. The Vice-Chancellor is currently away from the University, returning next week. In his absence I will make some enquiries with Professor Wrightson's office to try to establish what has happened to your application and revert as soon as possible.

Regards,

PA to the Vice-Chancellor

Enfield University

Dear Professor Grylls,

The VC has asked the Director of HR, Mike McDonagh, to respond to you on his behalf. I have sent a reminder email to Mr McDonagh this morning and asked him to revert to you as soon as possible.

Yours sincerely

PA to the Vice-Chancellor

Enfield University

I email this latest missive from the VC's office to a friend who taught at Enfield many years ago. I ask for his advice.

Hi Vaughan,

Good to see that Enfield is keeping up its grand old tradition of misusing the English language. "Revert" of course means to return to a previous state – as in "Superman reverted to Clark Kent". So quite what she has in mind when she says she's asked Mr McDonagh "to revert to you as soon as possible", I can't imagine. I also love the idea of your letter being "received into" the VC's office.

Now I must revert to washing up.

Dear Professor Grylls

Your letter of 18 April 2013 has been passed to me by the Vice-Chancellor, Professor John Sherbert, to investigate.

As I understand the situation, you applied for and were shortlisted for the post of Professor in Contemporary World Practices in Art, and invited to an interview on Thursday 28 March 2013. You were unable to attend an interview on that day as you were away in Italy and so it was arranged to interview you via Skype. Unfortunately on the day the Skype connection did not work and the interview panel were unable to call you. You telephoned the University and obtained the University's Skype address but were still unable to make the connection. You received an answerphone message from Heather Wrightson, Dean of School, informing you that the interview panel were trying to contact you, and you did try to call back but were not able to ring her back as ringback was not available on the number. You again tried to call the University but were not put through to the interview panel.

You emailed Heather on 28 March and 18 April to enquire about the next step but you did not receive a reply. Therefore you wrote to the Vice-Chancellor on 28 April. You have written to the Vice-Chancellor because you are unhappy that you were not informed of the outcome of the recruitment process by the University which you consider to be unprofessional as you undertook work and expense in preparation for the interview.

I have spoken to Heather and I understand that the interview panel did try to contact you via Skype at the allotted time but were unable to. They also telephoned you and left a voicemail message but eventually they had to move on. As you may be aware, the University is undertaking a large volume of recruitment at the moment and therefore it was not possible to arrange an alternative time for your interview. I understand that Heather did email you on 1 May and apologised for the fact that she had not replied to your emails.

It was very unfortunate that technology combined with the pressure of time conspired against us on the day and your interview was unable to take place. I know this was disappointing for you; however, I am sure that you will appreciate that these circumstances were beyond our control and I am satisfied that the interview panel made several attempts to contact you at the allotted time both via Skype and telephone. Notwithstanding that, the fact that you were not contacted following the conclusion of the recruitment process to inform you of the outcome was regrettable and I apologise for it.

I note that you arranged for a fast internet connection in Italy in preparation for the Skype call. Should you wish to be reimbursed for this expense please kindly forward your bank account details and cost of the Skype connection to Pamela Plaine, Office Manager of Human Resource Services, in order that she can arrange for a BACs transfer to your account to reimburse you for this.

Please be assured that it is our aim that best practice for recruitment is followed at all times within the University and I am sorry that the process did fall below the standards we would normally expect and to which all candidates are entitled on this occasion.

Yours sincerely

Mike McDonagh

Director of HR

This, of course, was little more than my complaint copied out and returned to me. At least he added an apology, although I hope Mr McDonagh will not, at some future date, revert to me or me to him.

GREAT ORMOND STREET HOSPITAL, 2016

Since Hattie was discharged from Great Ormond Street we have tried to put something back. At first we took part in street collections and things like that but when the opportunity arose for me to represent parents on the interview panels for new consultants at the hospital, I jumped at the chance. In 2015 Great Ormond Street Hospital for Children needed more Lay Chairs for their interview panels for consultants as they were expanding the hospital. I decided to apply.

"Good morning Vaughan. We're ready to see you now. Please come this way."

I follow the HR guy down a short corridor and into his office. Through the window I can see a corner of Queen Square. Sitting at a small round table with a plastic cup of water in front of each are the acting Medical Director and the Lay Chair of many interviews I have represented parents at. Two women and one man , whom I've just followed into this room. I know each of them. Is that a good thing?

The HR guy takes the third and beckons me to the fourth.

"We seem to see you a lot of you here at the moment."

"Yes. Perhaps I should start bringing in my sleeping bag."

"Ha ha! Water?"

"No, thank you."

"Well. Let's get started. Just from an HR perspective, what do you feel you could bring to this role?"

Straight in. No waffle. I like it.

"Expertise at interviewing and appointing people to senior posts – heads of school positions, professorships, albeit in art, design or architecture. But also heads of back office functions – finance, HR, student services, marketing. Just as important as the academics."

He smiles and nods.

"You did it for many years."

"I did. Seven at Walsall. Nine at Kent."

"So, I'd be interested to know what you thought of the presentations we in HR delivered last week explaining the role and responsibilities to the candidates. You would have been familiar with quite a lot of what we said."

"That is true. I could have answered some of the questions they raised myself. But not all. Not, for example, what it actually feels like to be a Lay Chair interviewing consultants."

I turn to the Lay Chair. I feel reassurance when she smiles and nods. Why do I still need that at this time in my life?

"And the tour of the hospital after the presentations?"

"Well, yes. I hadn't actually been in some of the places we visited since our daughter was here as a patient in 1995."

"You saw St Christopher's Chapel? Wonderful, isn't it?"

"Yes. I hadn't been in since that time. Beautiful Byzantine-inspired decoration. Designed by a son of Charles Barry, I think, who was one of the architects of the Houses of Parliament. A Victorian *tour de force*. Remarkable."

"How is your daughter?"

"Hattie? She's twenty-three now. Actually, we saw her off to a new job in Sydney, Australia, yesterday. One of those life-defining moments. You know."

I chuckle. They chuckle. What I don't say is that when I was shown into the chapel I had to slip into the corridor rather smartly before the others saw me with tears rolling down my face. It just all came back without warning. That real fear.

The HR guy turns to the acting Medical Director. It is her turn.

"What do you think is the most important part of the job of a Lay Chair, Vaughan?"

"Fairness. Ensuring fairness."

"Can you expand?"

"Yes. Fairness to each candidate. So they are treated equally, put at their ease, encouraged, especially if they are nervous. An internal candidate may be advantaged, as they almost certainly will know members of the interviewing panel and therefore may be better equipped to anticipate the questions. But a doctor who has never worked at Great Ormond Street may be disadvantaged. The hospital does not want to give the impression that it is much more likely to give a consultancy to a candidate who works here already. If that became the general perception, it could dissuade some good external candidates from applying. Some of the central London art colleges made that mistake in the 1970s and 1980s. It was an unfortunate perception."

Oh dear. I could be talking about myself. I've been on panels here for many years. The other seven candidates haven't. And it is a veiled criticism. Oh, well. Too late.

"H'mm. What about the interviewing panel?

"The same. Fairness. Ensuring some do not dominate at the expense of others. Or second guess the panel."

"Such as when?"

"Such as bringing extra information about a candidate to the panel after all the interviews are over and we are deciding who to appoint. That would be ruled out in a court of law, of course. But sometimes members of interview panels actually do that. A bit naughty."

"What about psychometric tests?"

The Lay chair has pitched in. I know she doesn't like them – in fact, she said as much at HR's presentations last week. But HR types absolutely love them. Careful, Vaughan.

"Er, well, it depends how and when the results are presented. And their status."

"Status?"

"Yes. They can be an important input. As are the references. But they are just that. An input to be considered. The main information is the interview itself and what the panel thinks about that."

Did I see a slight grimace from the HR guy?

"On one occasion when I was on the interviewing panel the results of a psychometric test were tabled by a member of the panel who would be the head of department to the appointee. He did it at the end of the discussion, using the results to try to change the panel's mind on the best candidate. He said that his colleagues who conducted the test had mandated him to let us know that they would not work with anyone but that candidate. Our Lay Chair, quite rightly I thought, stuck to his guns and asked us to go away and reflect and reconvene a few days later. We ended up appointing the candidate we had agreed on. Well, all of us except one. If a psychometric test alone is allowed to decide, the interview panel could become nothing more than a rubber stamp for decisions made by a department."

The acting Medical Director nods. The HR guy remains impassively silent. But it is back to her.

"Vaughan, why do you think that happened?"

"Well, I've seen it many times before. Not here. But it's understandable. The department to whom the successful candidate will be appointed wants someone who can 'hit the ground running' as they say. Someone who will fit the bill straightaway. But the institution is not just looking for straightaway. They should also be looking at the day after tomorrow. What is the candidate's potential to grow and, by extension, grow the institution? You could be looking at a future . . . Medical Director, perhaps? Many years ahead, of course."

"Oh. Yes. Of course. Now what about shortlisting? I had a case when we were shortlisting and a consultant came to see me to ask why we hadn't shortlisted a candidate he had recommended. I had to ring the Lay Chair of the panel."

The Lay Chair nods in agreement.

"And?"

"She backed me up. How would you respond?"

"Exactly the same. As Medical Director you have the whole hospital to consider. Not just a department and a favoured candidate. It sounds like a prequel to what I was talking about before."

"Thank you. I don't think I have any more questions."

It is finally the Lay Chair's turn. She comes to the salient point.

"I have just one question, Vaughan. Can you tell us why you applied for this job? From a personal perspective?"

"Yes. Two things really. I want to give something back to Great Ormond Street for saving Hattie's life and to apply my experience in doing so."

"And the second?"

"Well, an artist's life is a necessarily solitary one, whether you are a painter, sculptor, composer, writer. I have to put up with that so I can concentrate for periods of time. But I hate having to do it. The truth is the solitary life does not fit my personality. I love interacting with people. It is as simple as that."

She smiles. "Yes, I know what you mean. I have a son who is a composer."

This is the only interview I've ever had about interviews. But it is now at the end. So as I get up, and shake hands, I decide. I shall not apply for any more jobs or attend any more interviews. This must be the absolute last.

"Is this a convenient time to talk? For your debrief?"

"Yes. I thought I should ask for it. I was a bit taken aback by the phone call."

"Disappointment, of course. It is natural."

"No, er, yes. But not just that."

"What was it, particularly?"

"Well, being phoned by someone from HR who wasn't even on the interview panel. Seeing as we always require one of the panel to personally inform and debrief the unsuccessful candidates as well as the successful one."

"Oh. I think our HR representative said he was busy and he must have delegated informing the candidates."

"All seven of them?"

"Yes."

"Did you appoint any of the others, then?"

"No. Only one with current chairing experience. A civil servant."

"Well, I have to say, I don't think it gives a very good impression, especially as they have all just been interviewed about how to conduct interviews. Anyway, why didn't I get a job as a Chair?"

"Well . . . it was just that, the thing was the team felt you were too, er, gentlemanly."

"Gentlemanly?"

"Yes. Too gentlemanly to deal with strong-minded consultants. And we were looking for someone with current experience."

"Isn't gentlemanly and lack of current experience code for 'too old and out of touch'?"

"Well, I wouldn't go so far . . . "

I never heard any more about this interview, probably because I had hit the nail on the head!

CODA, 2017

There's an old guy, standing in the doorway of the conference room, humming to himself.

"Excuse me, sir. Can I help you?"

"Sorry. I was just leaving. Just popped in to see how much has changed. A lot. But the frieze round the building seems the same."

"Sir, this is an international student hostel. Private property."

"Of course. I'm leaving now."

I'll walk him to the front door. The last thing I need at the end of the day is a nutter standing around humming.

"I'm sorry I bothered you."

"No problem, sir. You take care now."

I'll stand here on the steps. You can never tell with nutters, even ones like him, now cycling off.

A bell tolls the hour at St Paul's.